ON THE CORRIDORS OF POWER: THE THEATRE OF THE ABSURD

ON THE CORRIDORS OF POWER: THE THEATRE OF THE ABSURD

PARIMAL BRAHMA

PARTRIDGE

To order additional copies of this book, contact
Partridge India
000 800 10062 62
orders.india@partridgepublishing.com

www.partridgepublishing.com/india

Contents

By Way of Preface

The moment I stepped on the corridors of South Block, I could sense power, smell power and see power. The long sandstone corridors flitted by the military top brass, diplomats and bureaucrats had been so imposing that for a moment, I thought Mao Zedong was wrong in saying that power flows from the barrels of the gun; I felt power flowed from the chessboard corridors of South Block and North Block! South Block houses the key ministries of Defence and External Affairs and North Block the Home Ministry and Finance Ministry. Traditionally, the Prime Minister has his office in South Block making it the main centre of sovereign power.

Political powers conferred by the Constitution and by the millions of electorates to the people's representatives are to be used for the public good and not for arrogating powers to the elected representatives. It is said that in a true democratic set up, *there is no real power unless there is misuse of power.* Unfortunately, with few exceptions, the people's representatives became more and more powerful and individual centres of power making the common people more and more helpless. The people started becoming cynical and apprehensive of their own representatives as the common citizens are about the Police who are supposed to protect them.

The most vulnerable and unenviable lot in the system had been the bureaucrats, especially the senior civil servants. Not always their fault but mainly their own making, the top bureaucrats made a total surrender and actively aided and abetted in the aggrandizement of the politicians in the growth of their personal wealth and power and in the process helped themselves with a few morsels. The majority of the top bureaucracy did very little to uphold the Constitution and help establish honesty, integrity and probity in public life conveniently sacrificing their oath to serve the nation in accordance with the Constitution without fear or favour. This would be amply demonstrated by one incident. Once I asked my Secretary 'who is the government?' He replied without any hesitation: 'as far as I am concerned, the Minister is the government.' I queried 'what if he is a corrupt minister and if he gives wrong orders?' His reply was: 'I am not supposed to question him and his integrity; I am here to implement his orders'.

From the beginning, I could realize that I was a misfit in the system. And most probably, my seniors and also my colleagues thought I was an idiot who could not understand the reality and refused to swim with the tide. I was neither capable of reaping benefits for myself from the system nor bestowing benefits to others by using my official position. I was accused of creating obstacles for others who wanted to make a clean sweep.

What has been the rightful place of the honest bureaucrats in the system? Practically, they are pushed to the corners in the system. They are tossed about, punished and side-tracked. The tragic story of Abhas Chatterjee who topped the Civil Services in 1966 remains a classic case of infinite capacity of politicians to destroy brilliant young bureaucrats when they do not compromise with their criminalities. Honest to the core, principled, straight forward, full of idealism and patriotism and bubbling with energy, Abhas never compromised on what was not right with any minister, politician or bureaucrat. He held on to his values and principles till his untimely death and set a glorious example of honesty and integrity. Luckily, the tribe of honest and upright bureaucrats was not extinct yet. I had the opportunity of knowing and working with a number of senior bureaucrats in the Central Secretariat who kept the *Satyameva Jayate* flag flying high. It was because of these few honest officers that the system did not collapse and moved on an elephantine pace.

I look back at my encounters in the Central Ministries with a sense of pride, a sense of fear, a sense of horror, a sense of helplessness and a sense of frustration. Being a non-conformist from childhood, I did not agree to compromise with any minister, politician or seniors on issues of principles and propriety. It became increasingly clear to me that no politician or a bureaucrat was interested in thinking of reforms, doing things for public good and serving people with patriotic fervour. Greed and power had overtaken almost every politician making them arrogant, revengeful and fearful people, and a genre of superior species that had no connection with the common people.

The idea of service to the nation with humility and patriotism evaporated after the death of the great Prime Minister, Lal Bahadur Shastri who was India's true 'people's Prime Minister'.

In this book, I have tried to highlight the funnier side of bureaucracy and capture the most humorous moments in my captivity and in the process, a number of serious issues, follies and absurdities, narrowness and selfishness, and lack of concern for the people and the nation on the part of the people in power have been brought out. I must make it abundantly clear that I have not consulted, quoted or resorted to any classified document or secret file of the government; the stories are all my personal reflections and interpretations as a participant- observer in the drama. I have revealed nothing new; the matters discussed were already in the public domain and which could easily be obtained under the RTI Act.

I often laugh at myself finding that for not doing anything worthwhile for the people and only for pushing files with arguments and counter-arguments for nearly four decades, even 'idiots' like me receive the highest pension from the government. What a waste of tax payer's money!

Parimal Brahma
New Delhi

Chapter One

Defence In Who's Hands –
Straw Men Or Stuffed Men!

I

Defence Scandals and Bofors:
An Alternative View

Where has been the beginning and the end of defence scandals? There cannot be any definitive answer. But one thing is certain: there will always be corruption and scandals where there is big money. And defence deals usually involve huge money, sometimes involving billions of dollars.

Post- independence, the first major defence scandals occurred during Nehru's regime. The Comptroller and Auditor General, Narahari Rao unearthed two scandals in the UK, which also appeared in the Audit Reports as the Jeep scandal and the Gun Powder scandal. V.K. Krishna Menon, the Indian High Commissioner, was found to be involved in both the scandals which took place not because he did anything for his personal gain but because of his arrogance and refusal to subject himself to any scrutiny and in-depth analysis. This greatly embarrassed Nehru's Government but in spite of the Audit Reports available in the Parliament, nothing happened to him and Menon was brought back by Nehru as the country's Defence Minister because he happened to be one of Nehru's greatest friends and advisors. And the nation had to pay a heavy price for Nehru's blind faith in him because Menon was largely responsible for the debacle in the Chinese War, 1962.

Since 1962, defence scandals were on low key and nothing came to the surface till the Bofors story broke out in April 1986. AB Bofors of Sweden has been a much maligned company following CAG's revelations about the kickbacks in the Bofors gun deal for the Indian Army. CAG's Audit Report rocked the Parliament and ultimately, led to the fall of Rajiv Gandhi Government. The scandal, believed to be the biggest corruption scandal till that time was originally revealed by the investigative journalism of Chitra Subramanian of *The Indian Express* and N. Ram of *The Hindu*, much before CAG's Office got a sense of it. CBI investigations and court trials were initiated which continued for nearly two decades without any conviction. One of the accused middlemen, Ottavio Quattrocchi, an Italian businessman reportedly close to the Gandhi family, stole the limelight all the time for his flamboyance and extreme cleverness to escape from the long arms of law in India, Malaysia, UK and Argentina. In spite of all efforts of the Indian intelligence agencies and international efforts, technical and legal flaws, believed to be deliberately created, enabled him to escape certain arrest and extradition to India for trials. Legal flaws and delays in taking action also enabled him to withdraw the kick-back money from the London banks in spite of court orders for freezing his bank account. The entire episode is shrouded in mystery and deceit.

Bofors suffered tremendously; they were black-listed in India for a very long time and their operations in India had to be suspended. The question naturally arose - did they deserve this? Or were they a victim of a corrupt political system? The answer perhaps is not far to seek.

Bofors had long been a leader in international export of defence equipment. They were one of the most reputed suppliers of defence equipment to the Indian Armed Forces for decades but nobody ever heard of kickbacks involving this company.

I had a fair share of dealings with Bofors. Till the end 1970s, I did not encounter any question or doubt about the defence deals with Bofors nor did I come across any criticism against the company in any of the Audit Reports of the CAG on the Defence Services.

This was because the dealings with Bofors and other major transnational companies were absolutely transparent. The procedure followed was like this. The Headquarters office would conduct technical evaluation of weapons and equipment and identify sources of supply. They would also invite initial offers for their requirements from the technically suitable sources and send the complete proposal to the Ministry for further negotiations and finalization of contract with the foreign firm. Invariably, the foreign firm will have an authorized Indian Agent in India, who is registered and recognized by the Ministry as the authorized Representative of the firm for the purpose of negotiations, clarifications and assistance but mainly to serve as the linkman for liaison work with the Principals located abroad. The Local Representative was officially permitted (it formed part of the contract) to accept an Agent's commission for the services rendered in India ranging from 2 to 5 percent of the contract value payable by cheque in Indian Rupees. This was a transparent and clean arrangement as it was white money on which the Agent was liable to pay taxes in India.

In the case of Bofors, their Indian Agent or Representative had been Anatronic Corporation of which Win Chadha was the sole owner. Today, people would find very hard to believe that Win Chadha, as my colleagues and I found him, had been a straight forward rich NRI and an honourable man. Win Chadha who had vast experience of defence supplies in USA was the Indian Representative of a number of foreign defence establishments including AB Bofors of Sweden. He had a well equipped air-conditioned office at Vasant Vihar, an air-conditioned luxury car (rare those days) and a few skilled staff. He had specialized in the field of supply of weapons and equipment for all the branches of the Armed Forces. Always elegantly dressed in suits, he had been a smart man who established cordial relations with all the concerned officers in the Army, Navy and Air Force Headquarters as well as officers of the Ministry of Defence. In the absence of computers those days, it was an uphill task to type out fair copies of contracts running into several hundred pages within a tight schedule. This task Win Chadha used to do ungrudgingly as part of his 'services' to his principals. Every time amendments or corrections were made to the main contract, he would rush to his office and in no time would come back with the fair copies neatly typed in his electronic typewriters. Sometimes, he would be harassed with last minute changes and alternations, but I never found him reluctant to the task of bringing out fresh copies of the contract. During my entire tenure, Win Chadha did not try to give a gift after the contracts were signed and the same thing applied to other colleagues of the Ministry. Once, he invited some of us to a dinner at Ashoka Hotel hosted in honour of senor functionaries of AB Bofors who visited India to sign a contract. Obviously, we politely refused. The following incident will illustrate the straight forward approach of the man. On a New

Year day, a tall attractive girl enters my room and offers a packet saying it was from Anatronic Cooperation, Win Chadha's firm. I asked her to open it, which she did and I found there was a New Year Diary and a pen set. I kept the Diary and refused the pen-set but the girl hesitated to take it back saying that 'I have orders to hand over the packets and not to take back anything'. I said 'fair enough'. I picked up the telephone and rang up Win Chadha asking him if he would get the pen-set collected or I should sent it back with an official note from me. He apologized for the episode and promised to collect it next day, which he did. Thereafter, Win Chadha did not send or offer any gift item, not even the customary New Year diary or calendar.

The Swedish Laws prohibited their own Enterprises to adopt any corrupt practice (to secure contracts etc) in their business operations. AB Bofors did maintain a very high standard of business ethics and during my days in the Defence Ministry, Bofor's possible involvement in bribery or corruption was almost unthinkable. I was not aware if Bofors offered even token gifts on conclusion of contracts with them.

The only valuable gift I received during my entire tenure in Defence Ministry was a golden Parker ball pen presented during the signing ceremony of an infamous contract with M/s Westland Helicopters. I did not have any alternative in this case because protocol niceties demanded that no gift presented by a foreign delegation in an official ceremony should be refused. The practice was any expensive gift received by any Government official within the country or in a foreign country should be sent to 'Toshakhana'(a valuation Cell of the Ministry of External Affairs) for valuation and if the value exceeded Rs. 250 those days, permission of Government of India should be obtained for its retention by the individual officer. Else, it should be deposited to the Government as Government property. So, I promptly wrote a personal note to my Joint Secretary requesting him to approach 'Toshakhana' in the Ministry of External Affairs to determine the value of the golden Parker ball pen and also to decide if the gift can be retained by me. Promptly, the note came back with the reply saying that I may retain the gift. I was rather surprised.

Then I understood that my Joint Secretary who rose from the ranks of stenographers in the Central Secretariat (a great achievement) did not wish to approach *Toshakhana* because he himself retained his gift of an electronic pad (a rare possession those days) without consulting Toshakhana. I was unhappy because I never accepted any costly gift, but I thought I should not embarrass him by writing to him again and gifted the ball pen to my wife. The other time I was offered a gift was when I was a member of a committee for revision of prices of Ships which were under construction at Garden Reach Shipbuilders

Engineers (GRSE), Calcutta. GRSE, a Public Sector Undertaking approached the Ministry asking them to revise the prices of the ships because of rising costs and delays and unless the prices were increased, they could not proceed with the work of construction of the ships. A three-member committee was dispatched to Calcutta to 'pacify' GRSE. While the other two members were lodged in Grand Hotel, but I preferred to stay at my parental house at Dumdum from where it was very difficult to commute daily to Garden Reach. On conclusion of a tedious task, GRSE sent to each member of the committee a gift pack containing an electronic pad, a new thing which came in the market. I politely refused but my other colleges retained the gift pack. Because of incidents like this, I was a subject of ridicule and was branded 'hyper-sensitive' by my colleagues in the Ministry. One colleague commented that I need not be paranoid about gifts and should not extend the issue to a ridiculous limit. I said I was trained by and therefore, was a disciple of M.G. Pimputkar (Director, National Academy), who used to keep two fountain pens in his pocket- one pen for official use filled in ink supplied by the office and another pen filled with ink purchased by him for his personal use. For writing anything which is not official, he would take out his personal pen. This is the moral standard he set for all officers in the National Academy. I said I was trying to follow the government rule only.

Coming back to the Westland Helicopters deal, to my mind, this was a far greater scandal than the Bofors gun deal and it is amazing that while there was national and international outcry about the Bofors deal, there was no ripple in any forum about the Westland deal. Westland Helicopters were on the brink of bankruptcy when he British Government drew up a plan to rescue the company. Since the British laws did not allow them to give direct subsidy to a private company, the British Government, therefore, devised a novel plan to bail out the company. The prototype was still under development and the helicopters were not test flown. There was an ongoing development aid programme launched by UK on the pattern of US-AID programmes in India. An agreement was reached (innocently agreed to by the Indian Prime Minister without knowing the ulterior motive of the British Government) between the two Prime Ministers under which India would buy a batch of helicopters from Westland (already a sinking company) and an equivalent amount in Pound Sterling would be transferred to India under the UK aid programmes. The helicopters were not perfectly air-worthy and after a series of accidents, the entire fleet was grounded. The entire money went down the drain. It was practically a fraud committed on India as the helicopters were never operational.

In sharp contrast, the world did not fail to notice that Bofors never compromised on quality, cutting edge technology and sophistication, which had been the hall-mark of Bofors.

The people of India should be grateful to Bofors because it is the Bofors guns which won the Kargil war for us. But for the technological superiority and greater fire-power of the Bofors guns, Pakistan could have won the war. And the victory over Pakistan was possible only because of the infamous gun-deal.

The million-dollar question is why and how did AB Bofors get involved in the business of kickbacks? I was not in the picture. But I can guess, based on my past experiences with Bofors, that it all happened because of excessive greed and unholy migration from a transparent system of defence deals to a non-transparent non-system, which caused the back-lash leading to untold misery. Over-greed forced the existing power-structure to commit the folly of abolishing the system of Indian Agency of foreign firms and the established system of payment of a limited amount of legalized commission to them in white money. Abolition of the system opened the doors of unscrupulous manipulations in garnering commissions in black money. Bofors were perfectly happy in legally paying a small percentage of the contract value to Win Chadha who would look after their interests in India as Bofors representative bear the costs of processing the deals and the cost involved in the visits of their delegations to India. With the abolition of the Indian Agents system, Bofors could not have effectively carried on their operations in India without opening a new office, which would have been an expensive and impractical proposition. So, Win Chadha continued to operate unofficially as the sole Agent of Bofors. There must have been greater demands on Bofors to shell out a much greater percentage (may be more than 10%) of the contract value of the Gun deal as "commission" and Win Chadha must have been forced to shell out the major part of the unusually high amount of the commission money and serve as a the conduit for transfer of funds to the interested parties in their foreign accounts. Here enters the most charismatic actor of the drama, Ottavio Quattrocchi who (I can only guess) must have played his role perfectly as a middleman for securing a high percentage of commission in foreign currency and transferring the foreign funds directly to the Swiss banks. My interpretation of the episode is that both Win Chadha and AB Bofors could have been the victims of manipulations, unscrupulousness and greed of Indian politicians and they were virtually 'trapped' without an escape route. In the process, Win Chadha not being able to take any more harassment lost his life. AB Bofors suffered immeasurably, lost their good brand image, senior functionaries disgraced and above all, lost the lucrative Indian business for more than a decade. No intelligent organization will risk this willingly.

The charge sheets submitted in the Indian Courts included the name of a former Prime Minister of India,

Rajiv Gandhi. I find it hard to believe that such a straight-forward and charismatic leader liker Rajiv Gandhi who, I am sure, would have been a great Prime Minister of India had he been alive, would get himself involved in this dirty game. Again I feel, he must have been trapped by his ill-advised advisors who thought defence contracts were a goldmine which remained to be tapped and that instead of droplets of funds contributed by Indian industrialists who would again demand their pound of flesh after the elections, the Party kitty will overflow with the "contributions" received from a few major defence deals. But the methods they followed were wrong. Unfair means remain unfair and always boomerang, which the advisors realized too late. Meanwhile, the image of the Defence Ministry was tarnished and the morale of the Armed Forces was substantially affected. It was very difficult to heal the wounds.

Bofors gun deal had not been the first case of defence scandal. In the 1950s, the famous Gun Powder Scandal was revealed in CAG's Audit Reports which created quite a commotion in Parliament and outside. Krishna Menon was involved in the scandal but Nehru defended Menon arguing that Krishna Menon could never have any personal interest and it occurred due to lack of vigilance on the part of the India Supply Mission in UK. It is quite possible that the usual arrogance, personal preference for a particular firm and lack of knowledge of the technicalities of the deal could have landed him in trouble but it was unthinkable to assume that he was personally responsible for the gun powder not firing or that any financial benefit had been passed on to him. But the situation in Bofors case had been totally different. Here, there was a deliberate conspiracy orchestrated by the politicians to cheat the government and commit third-degree corruption.

II

Strategic Projects – One Two Three Infinity!

Many of the projects I had been handling had been conceived in 1950s and 1960s; still, their completion was never in sight. As if they were designed to go on in perpetuity, the projects went on and on – funds would be allotted every year, new managers would take over charge and old managers would be transferred on promotion. Nobody seemed to have accountability for no-execution, failures and wastage of public funds.

This had precisely been the main concern of the CAG; in one of his reports, he made a scathing criticism of the Naval Dockyard Project at Bombay for lack of proper survey, lack of proper project report, non-realistic time schedule, inordinate delays in execution, cost-overrun, non-performance and utter lack of commitment. The Project which started in 1960s with a target of 3 years for phase-I and another 2 years for phase-II merrily continued for two decades!

This was an extremely serious Audit paragraph in the Defence Report of the CAG. But, as usual, nobody in the Defence Ministry noticed it, least of all read it until a notice was received from the Lok Sabha Secretariat that this Paragraph had been selected for oral evidence in the public Accounts Committee (PAC). The Secretariat also sent an unusually lengthy questionnaire containing about one hundred questions and asking for replies to the questions to be sent within four weeks.

The fate of CAG's Audit Reports is only too well-known. Every year, a number of Audit Reports are received from the CAG and after cursory look by the Secretary; the Reports are marked down through a number of levels to the Under Secretary who consign them to old records without being read and without any action thereon. The PAC had been one authority all Ministries were mortally afraid of.

So the Defence Ministry woke up from slumber on receiving the questionnaire on the Naval Dockyard Project. I fact, on close reading of the Audit Para, all senior officials including the Defence Secretary were literally shocked and wondered how on earth such a terrible mess was allowed to go on by the Project authorities, the Navy Headquarters and the Ministry itself. But the problem arose as to who would prepare effective replies to the questionnaire since none of the senior officers had any idea about the background of the project. Ultimately, as usual, the entire responsibility of preparation of the draft replies for approval of the Defence Secretary fell on the poor under Secretary, i.e. me. But I had no knowledge of the issues nor had seen any paper on the subject to enable me to prepare an effective reply to any of the 100-odd questions. One of the main defects of the single-file system and frequent transfer of officers under the central staffing pattern had been that no 'memory' is developed and all memory disappears with the transfer of the officials. I was rescued by an experienced Accounts officer from the Defence Accounts Department, Mr. Banerjee who was on deputation to the Ministry as an additional help. Mr. Banerjee who had been a bachelor was assigned the task of marshalling all the facts and files and also to prepare the draft replies. Meanwhile, more time was asked for from the PAC Secretariat for furnishing the replies. It took about three months for the Ministry to finalize the replies and as far as my Division was concerned, all other work virtually stopped. It was amazing that Mr. Banerjee could dig out about 400 files from the old records and put up draft replies to at least one or two questions along with the bundles of supporting papers everyday for Defence Secretary's approval.

The day all the replies were finalized and dozens of cyclostyled sets were taken out, I finally heaved a sigh of relief and without waiting for a moment, I rang up the Financial Committee officer, a junior service colleague and 'originator' of this 'Mahabharat', asking if I could personally come and deliver the papers to him. I remember it was lunch time and there was not a soul in the section except one handicapped helper who had difficulties in going out for lunch. I requisitioned an Army Car, brought down the bundles of papers from the fifth floor with the help of the lone helper, drove to Parliament House Annex and handed over the heaps of papers to him. Instead of thanking me for meeting the deadline and for taking the trouble of personally carrying the heavy bundles to him and offering a cup of tea, started elaborating his own achievements, how cleverly he could frame the questions to make things difficult for the Ministry and how the Chairman, PAC could be impressed by his 'monumental' work. In the evening, I was a much relieved person and for the first time in many months, shared lighter moments with my family. I also promised my wife that we would certainly make a programme to go to the children's park at the India Gate.

But, this was not the end of the story. Very soon, intimation was received that Defence Secretary had been summoned to give oral evidence before the PAC on the same Audit Para; obviously, the replies to the questionnaire, so laboriously prepared, did not satisfy the Committee. Moreover, very unusually, the oral evidence was slated over two full days. Again, the whole Ministry went into a mode of fire fighting - rounds of notes, discussions, examination and re-examination, meetings and feverish activity.

For two full days, the Defence Secretary along with the senior officers of the Ministry and of the Project, were thoroughly grilled by the Chairman and the Members of the PAC. While I had practically no role during the proceedings except marking my nervous presence, I had thoroughly enjoyed the debate. What made the entire hall spellbound was the extraordinary oratorical power of the Chairman, Prof. Hiren Mookerjee, an outstanding Parliamentarian of his time. His skill and humour brought many smiles in an otherwise extremely grim situation when the whole Ministry was on the mat. I was also little amused and happy to see that the ammunition provided by the CAG's representatives to the Chairman 'fired' much better and pierced through the 'defence' of the Defence Ministry. The Defence Secretary, Mr. D.R. Kohli, very proud of his ICS tag and rather contemptuous of other 'not so heavenly born' Service colleagues, after two days of verbal onslaught, looked totally deflated. After this episode, I was told his shouting at the meetings of officers assumed some sobriety. Had there been Mr. Govind Narain (whom he succeeded) in his place, I am sure, things would have been totally different. Mr. Govind Narain who had the goodwill and reputation of deft handling of such matters, would have, with his inimitable style, certainly taken the PAC into confidence and perhaps, the PAC discussions would have happily ended in one session instead of spreading over two days.

A few months later, the PAC report containing their recommendations was submitted to the parliament and was received in the Ministry for implementation. The stout defence put up by the Defence Ministry during the oral evidence had the opposite effect and the PAC Report submitted to Parliament was more devastating than the Audit Report itself, couched in stronger language and containing more scathing criticism of the Ministry. Action taken notes on the implementation of each of the recommendations were to the furnished by the Ministry to the PAC within a period six months. Fortunately for me, I did not continue as Under Secretary that long and was saved from another gruelling drill.

III

Arbitration for 14 years!

The Indian Arbitration Act envisaged arbitration proceedings to be completed and award issued within a time-limit of four months; reasonable extension could be given depending on the complexity of the case. One of the main criticisms of the CAG's Audit Report on the Naval Dockyard Project had been the conduct of arbitration proceedings which extended beyond 14 years.

A retired Chief Justice of High Court had been appointed by the Ministry as the sole arbitrator in a contractual dispute between a foreign contract firm from Yugoslavia and the Dockyard Project authorities. Considering that the Arbitrator had been a retired Judge, the Ministry could not perhaps question the reasonability of lingering the arbitration proceedings. It is only when the CAG's Audit Party started questioning the wisdom of continuing indefinitely with the arbitration; the proceedings were hurriedly brought to close. Meanwhile, the Law Ministry had merrily granted about 60 extensions to the arbitrator spanning over 14 years. Perhaps, this had been the longest arbitration case of its kind in India deserving a place in the Guinness Book of Records!

The irony of the matter was that while the award was given in favour of the Government, the Government had spent much more money on the arbitration than the amount awarded in its favour. Had the Ministry negotiated the demand of the foreign firm without going for arbitration, it would have saved enormous amount of public funds, energy and time. After the Defence Ministry and the Law Ministry were pulled up by the PAC, a system of quarterly monitoring of all arbitration cases of the central Government was introduced by the Ministry of Law which is perhaps still continuing till today.

IV

Sardar Swaran Singh – 'Bureaucrat of all Bureaucrats'

When I joined the Ministry of Defence in 1974, the Defence Minister had been Sardar Swaran Singh. He was known as 'the bureaucrat of all bureaucrats'. As the Defence Minister, Mr. Swaran Singh did not perhaps require a Defence Secretary because he was capable of doing the combined work of the Secretary and the Minister. He could give a good reading of the files, examine the proposals thoroughly, verify the facts and the situations, weigh pros and cons of the proposals and give a balanced decision with a clear speaking order. His decisions were always on the basis of the merits of the proposals and not on political considerations. In fact, he never played politics in the Ministry. A soft-spoken, lean and lanky Sikh, Sardar Sahib's behaviour with the officials was immaculate; he never made anybody small. He was not feared, rather loved by all and he commanded respect from everybody. Sardar Sahib had been a perfect example of a gentleman politician – a tribe which vanished soon from the Indian political scene.

One fine morning, the whole Ministry was shocked to know that this gentleman politician had been shifted out of the Defence Ministry; rather, he had been removed from the Union Cabinet. News also trickled in that Mrs. Indira Gandhi, the Prime Minister would be the new Defence Minister (Raksha Mantri) as an additional portfolio. I felt a pang of sadness, so also all my colleagues who were still dazed in utter disbelief. We were all sorry to lose this perfect gentleman. We were also asked to attend a farewell dinner thrown in by Mrs. Gandhi herself at Hyderabad House the same evening in 'honour' of Sardar Swaran Singh to be proceeded by a farewell meeting.

So all of us marched to Hyderabad House in the evening to bid farewell to the outgoing Defence Minister and also welcome the new Defence Minister (although it appeared to be a temporary arrangement). Mrs. Gandhi's speech was full of diplomatic platitudes; she underlined Sardar Sahib's great achievements as Defence Minister and said that his rich experience and services were required elsewhere for a greater purpose. Nothing much was heard of Sardar Swaran Singh in subsequent days of political turmoil.

Sardar Sahib could sense that this was the beginning of the end of his political career. In his heart he always wanted to be a bureaucrat rather than a politician. But he could not anticipate that a 'catastrophe' would befall on him so soon; no fault of his because nobody on earth could read Mrs. Gandhi's mind and her political moves. For the first time, we found that Sardar Sahib could not put up a smiling face (which was usual with him) and worries and sadness were largely writ on his appearance. He thanked Mrs. Gandhi for the 'great confidence' reposed on him. He particularly praised the officials of the Defence Ministry and that he had a wonderful time with them as friends. A statement of his still rings in my ears – 'you bureaucrats have an assured career, a settled life, but we politicians have only uncertainties and an uncharted life, which we cannot navigate on our own'. The country lost a great administrator.

The buzz on the corridors was that Mrs. Gandhi never wanted Sardar Swaran Singh to go but was forced to drop him from the Cabinet under pressure from one of his sons who was emerging as the most influential politician of the emergency era. He found Sardar Sahib an obstacle to his political and other ambitions and decided to replace him with a pliable minister who would take commands from him. It is Swaran Singh's honesty, integrity and adherence to rules which brought his downfall.

V

The Wrong Dinner Plate!

After the farewell party, the dinner party began. Defence Ministry being a very large Ministry, the number of officers present were also large. All were introduced to the new Prime Minister-cum-Defence Minister. The dinner was laid out on the open lawns of Hyderabad House which belonged to the Ministry of External Affairs. Those days, the so-called modern security threats did not exist and VVIPs could move rather freely. At least, that evening, at Hyderabad House, I did not notice the 'Black Cats' or the gun-trotting security personnel anywhere. Mrs. Gandhi and Sardar Sahib were moving and talking freely in the crowd.

Hyderabad House located the Entertainment Division of the Ministry of External Affairs, which organized all official lunches and dinner hosted by the Prime Minister. This party was also organized by them. Pretty girls elegantly dressed in saris were serving the guests and Mrs. Gandhi being the host chose to wait till the queue ended along with few of us, still to pick up plates. She had been in a profusely cheerful mood and was telling some of her interesting experiences and while talking, picked up a plate for her frugal meal. Immediately, a girl of the Entertainment

Division rushed towards her and almost snatched the plate apologizing 'Madam, sorry this is not your plate'. She picked up another plate from a secret place and handed over to her. I was standing next to her and could notice her face turn almost red. Visibly embarrassed she said to the girl 'you should have told me earlier'. To make things lighter, she continued 'look, these people have made me a prisoner – I don't have the freedom to pick up a dinner plate!' She took a few morsels of food brought by the girls from a secret place on 'secret' plate.

I rushed home as soon as Mrs. Gandhi left Hyderabad House. Those days, it was almost impossible to get a public transport in the night from India Gate. Fortunately, some of us could pool together in a Defence vehicle. My wife was terribly worried. Since I did not have any home telephone those days, there was no means of sending a message to her. This particular evening at the Hyderabad House gave me quite a few lessons on Machiavellian diplomacy, on the psychology of people in absolute power and how beautifully political sacrifices of great personalities can be made with covert ruthlessness.

VI

Sheikh Mujibur Rahman – The Tiger of Bangladesh

The story of rise and fall of Sheikh Mujibur Rahman is one of the most fascinating and tragic stories of modern times. A towering personality, an undisputed leader of Bangladesh (then East Pakistan) 'Bangabandhu' Mujibur Rahman had all the making and charisma of a world leader – a dream unfortunately remained unfulfilled.

Sheikh Mujib galvanized the entire Bengali Speaking people of Pakistan to launch a movement for autonomy for East Bengal (then East Pakistan) and restoration of Bengali pride by making Bengali the official language of East Bengal instead of Urdu which was not understood by the common people. The 'Language Movement' started by students in Dacca University (now Dhaka), which had seen many bloody battles and brute suppressions, culminated into a full-scale autonomy movement. Sheikh Mujib became the unchallenged hero of the masses and his party, Awami League based on secular and democratic principles became the most popular political Front.

General Elections based on guided democracy were held for both the wings of Pakistan - Z.A. Bhutto of Pakistan Peoples' Party leading the West and Sheikh

Mujib of Awami Party leading the East – as part of a deal struck between the military junta and the political parties for restoration of democracy and popular governments in Pakistan. The results of the general elections were spectacular and most unexpected by the West. Mujib Rahman's Awami Party more than 90 percent of seats of East Pakistan and secured an absolute majority in The National Assembly of Pakistan at Islamabad. The results were not acceptable either to the military regime or Zulfikar Ali Bhutto who was assured and was himself certain about getting the post of Prime Minister of Pakistan. The possibility of Mujibur Rahman's becoming the Prime Minister of united Pakistan had to be eliminated because the administrators of West Pakistan and the military leaders who hated the Bengali Muslims as 'inferior' to them would never accept Mujib as PM. Pakistan was in a serious dilemma and they opted for an easy option they knew well -'crackdown'. So, there was an all- out military crackdown in East Pakistan. Martial Law was imposed and the election results for the East were declared null and void. The top leadership of Awami Party was put behind the bar and Mujib was arrested and deported to an unknown destination somewhere in West Pakistan on charges of sedition. An era of suppression, arrests and torture targeting the Hindus and the supporters of Awami Party began. The holocaust which followed the martial law was similar to Hitler's attempt to exterminate Jews in Poland. It was estimated that the Pakistan Army was responsible for killing 3 million Bengalis. The Army also resorted to a dastardly act of wiping out the entire top leadership and intellectuals after they were arrested and lodged in jails.

Bhutto and the military junta completely misread the situation after the elections. If Bhutto agreed to share power with Awami League and made Mujib the Prime Minister of Pakistan, even by rotation, the entire agenda of autonomy for East Bengal would have slowly died out. Secondly, Mujib could have been persuaded to remain in East Bengal ruling this part of the country (renamed as Bangladesh) as its President with maximum possible autonomy within a new federal structure of Pakistan. In that case, Bhutto could have ruled Pakistan as its Prime Minister with the support of Mujib's Party. Instead of working out a political solution which would also satisfy the aspirations of Bengalis, the leadership chose the path of extreme suppression, torture and bloodshed, which every Bengali rebelled against.

The holocaust cemented every Bengali's resolve for autonomy into a demand for full independence from West Pakistan's rule. It may be recalled that the genesis of the independence movement goes back to a simple and just movement for making Bengali as the official language for East Bengal and non-imposition of Urdu, a language not understood by the common Bengali, as the sole official language of East Pakistan. This was a fair demand which was mishandled and was suppressed with all military brutalities. This simple language movement led to demands for autonomy which gradually escalated into a movement for independence. It is a sad reflection on the attitudes of the administrators those days. The administrators in East Bengal with their arrogance, lack of human approach, lack of foresight and total lack of understanding of the feelings and needs of the local people precipitated the demise of Pakistan in East Bengal. Had they adopted a three language formula, an impartial administration, an independent judiciary and allowed a popular government to function, there would probably been no demand for independence from united Pakistan.

It is an irony of history (history never forgives!) that Bhutto who played into the hands of military rulers and was indirectly responsible for the holocaust in East Bengal himself became a victim of his own actions and designs. He was first condemned by the military for dismembering Pakistan, then sent to prison and later executed without a fair trial. His overthrow again by a military regime left a trail of suppression, destruction of all democratic institutions, violence and lack of freedom in West Pakistan.

Coming back to Mujib, nobody knew where he had been taken to. There were floating rumours about him including his being killed and no authentic information was forthcoming because all news about Mujib had been blacked out by the military junta. It was certain that Mujib had been flown out of Bengal. One speculation was he had been confined to a remote jail in Baluchistan. Another speculation was he had been killed and secretly buried in West Pakistan. The Indian intelligence agencies and for that matter no international agency including the KGB had any clue about his disappearance. Probably, the CIA knew about his whereabouts as it was subsequently known that the American President could have asked the military rulers to spare Mujib's life.

I have never believed in Astrology and have always considered Astrological predictions as probabilities. Yet, certain predictions approximated the truth with such flying colours and with such accuracy that you are often forced to believe: 'yes, there is something in it'. One of such rare predictions coming true concerned Mujib. One day, a colleague of mine brought a copy of Raman's Astrological Magazine and asked me to read the leading article dealing with Mujib's future. I still vividly remember the predictions made on Mujib's life by Raman: *the horoscope of Mujib shows he is very much alive; he will come out of prison unharmed and he will be the head of state of a new nation.* The accuracy of predictions like this leads people to develop blind faith in Astrology. But in my case, even if Raman's predictions proved correct to the extent of one hundred per cent, this could not displace my basic scepticism about Astrology.

The 'Mukti Bahini' (Liberation Army) of the exiled Government of Bangladesh trained and aided by the Indian Army entered Bangladesh from all sides and started swelling their ranks with the support and help of the local people who were prepared to fight the Pakistani Army. The refugee problem became extremely acute. Because of a policy of purging the Hindu population, refugees started overflowing on the Border States West Bengal, Assam, Meghalaya and Tripura. When the number of displaced persons exceeded 10 million who had to be given shelter and fed, Mrs. Indira Gandhi thought enough was enough and asked the Indian Armed Forces to enter Bangladesh by land, air and sea along with Mukti Bahini. When the paratroopers landed in Dacca, General Manekshaw used his famous trick asking the Pakistani Commanders to surrender as the Pakistani forces had been surrounded by the Indian troops from all sides and any fight would mean sure death. The trick worked, there was no fight and the entire Pakistani Army commanded by Lt. Gen. Niazi surrendered to the Indian Army. It was a bloodless coup and was perhaps the greatest victory of the Indian Armed Forces and the worst defeat of the Pakistani Army in military history as 91,000 soldiers of Pakistani Army surrendered who were taken to India as prisoners of war.

Mujib-ur-Rahman had a triumphant return to Dacca via New Delhi. After his release from exile, he wanted to meet Mrs. Indira Gandhi first whom he treated as his 'sister'. Especially, he wanted to meet her to express his gratitude and the gratitude of his people for the liberation of Bangladesh in an unprecedentedly swift move of Indian troops and also for saving his own life enabling him to lead Bangladesh again. Had there been no Indira Gandhi at the helm of affairs at that time, perhaps, there would have been no sovereign Bangladesh.

Mujib became the first head of government of independent Bangladesh. The new constitution declared Bangladesh as Secular Democratic Republic of Bangladesh, which no Muslim country in the world did except Turkey. After fresh elections in accordance with the new constitution of free Bangladesh, Mujib became the President. Mujib was declared the Father of the Nation and after a few years, the National Assembly made him President for Life. I thought Mujib would certainly decline the resolution to make him Life-President expecting him to have a good sense of history and also believing him as true democrat. History is replete with instances that any move like this invariably brought the downfall of the ruler.

Mujib overestimated his popularity and underestimated, rather totally ignored the threat perceptions. But the simmering discontent had been growing within his own Army, his own party and fellow freedom fighters. The pro- Pakistani and pro-Islamic elements converted this discontent into conspiracies to remove him. The pro-Islamic elements did not like his style of functioning and were upset with the concept of a secular state as they wanted an Islamic Republic of Bangladesh. This was the greatest cause which they wanted to achieve at any cost, even by sacrificing their Father of the Nation.

Sheikh Mujibur Rahman was blissfully unaware of this. But report about danger to his life started pouring in through foreign and Indian intelligence sources. The Indian Embassy had been sending reports, over a period of time, about dangers to Mujib's life. One day, I was shocked read a report from emanating from Dacca that a conspiracy had been hatched to kill Mujib and his family and that attack could be imminent. I still remember I wanted to transmit the news through normal channels to Mrs. Gandhi who had been then the Prime Minister as well the Defence Minister. She must have received similar reports from many other sources - the External Affairs Ministry, IB, and other Intelligence agencies. But no amount of such reports, warnings and India's intervention could save Mujib's life. Mujib and his entire family - his sons, daughters and grandchildren were brutally murdered by some of his Army Commanders. Three generations of the Mujib family were wiped out; only one of his daughters, Sheikh Hasina who had been out of the country at that time, escaped death. The hate was so strong that they wanted to completely obliterate Mujib's name and

Mujib's legacy. The cruelty and brutality perpetrated on their Father of the Nation was unparalleled in history. A similar instance is available in the Mahabharata where the *Pandava* sons were killed by Ashwathama in the middle of the night while they were sleeping. I was again reminded of Raman's Astrological prediction which was ominously silent on what would happen to Mujib after he became the head of the state.

Indira Gandhi was sad and quite shaken after this tragedy as she knew Bangladesh without Mujib would not be so friendly and in fact, with rising fundamentalism, could be worse than Pakistan as our neighbour. The freedom we fought for them was undone.

Mrs. Gandhi deeply felt for Mujib and both in public and private, regretted that in spite of her personal interventions on several occasions asking him to take adequate protection for himself and his family, Mujib ignored her warning and laughed it away. Every time, Mujib would dismiss such thoughts saying 'they are all my brothers and sisters, sons and daughters- how can they kill me? I can't imagine such a thing'. But his unshakable innocence and faith in human goodness, like Gandhiji's, helped the messengers of death to complete the heinous act. Mrs. Indira Gandhi also became a victim of the same act in the next decade when her own bodyguards gunned her down at her official residence after 'Operation Bluestar' ending another colourful chapter of history.

VII

Storm in the Water Glass

As Defence Minister, Mrs. Gandhi used to take important meetings in the historic War Room, a beautiful circular meeting room at the top of the central dome of South Block. Normally, an Under Secretary should not have any occasion to attend such meetings for which the minimum level was that of a Joint Secretary. Since the subject matter concerned my Desk and since I was working directly with the Joint Secretary without having a middle level supervision, my Joint Secretary, C.P. Ramachandran, an extremely affectionate boss who believed in his juniors getting maximum exposure, asked me to join him for the meeting. I resisted but failed. I was totally unprepared, extremely nervous and was sure I would perform miserably if any question of clarification arose or if I was asked to answer any question.

Entering the room, I felt that the aura and power of the room had taken away all powers of me. I felt terribly thirsty. I could feel the palpitations in my heart. I tried to reach out for a glass of water. Not finding any arrangement for drinking water within the room, I thought the water glasses must have been kept nicely near the windows behind the curtains. I rushed to one of the windows pulling a part of the thick curtains and stood shocked to see that I almost dashed against the bayonets of two commandos of the elite security force positioned there much earlier. I went to the second window and then to the third window and instead of getting a glass of water, I got the glimpses of Prime Minister's special protection group with rifles and other gadgets. But the entire group consisting of half a dozen chosen personnel did not move or utter a single word and silently pulled the curtains to make them invisible. It is possible that the Prime Minister herself did not know about their presence in the room.

On hearing some noises and sounds of footsteps, I quickly came back to my seat. Along with some dignitaries, Mrs. Gandhi entered the room like a gust of fresh air. In an off -white silk sari she was grace personified. She was in an unusually good mood smiling, laughing and cracking jokes. Her amicability diminished my fear and thirst but a glass of water would have restored my confidence.

A glass of water soon arrived, not for me but for Mrs. Gandhi. As had been the practice, all foods and drinks of PM are carefully screened, protected and handled by PM's personal staff. So, one of her personal attendants brought her special glass of water and placed it in between her and the Defence Secretary and also put a beautiful beaded laced cloth on top of it. My attention was focussed on the glass of water as I needed it most but had to be satisfied only by looking at it. Luckily, the proceedings did not linger on very much. Mrs. Gandhi did most of the talking and took a commanding position and people who asked questions were quickly silenced by her sharp replies. I could notice that the talkative Defence Secretary (Mr. Kohli) silenced during the session, was busy trying to fix the laced cloth which slipped from the top of the water glass. Since the laced cloth piece was heavy with beads on all sides, and was wrongly kept in four folds, became heavier on one side and quietly slipped off the glass. Mr. Kohli tried again and again to put the folded cloth on top of the glass but every time he put it, it slipped down. Mrs. Gandhi, even if she was busy explaining a point noticed it, casually took the folded cloth, opened it and placed it nicely on the glass top. It was like Christopher Columbus' fabled story of putting the egg vertically on the dinner plate! Mr. Kohli was visibly embarrassed; the 'mighty' ICS officer could not even fix a laced cloth on a glass of water even after repeated efforts! Those who noticed it felt amused. I felt like laughing and enjoyed the rebuff which remained a memorable small event in my life. Not surprisingly, Mrs. Gandhi did not need his 'assistance' throughout the deliberations which ended rather quickly. Without waiting for the usual pleasantries after the meeting was over, I ran down the stairs and the corridors and gulfed three glasses of water to cool me down.

VIII

Attempt to Escape

Every time I attempted to escape from the Defence Ministry, rather trying for a 'jail break,' I met with failure. The reason was I did not at all enjoy working in the Defence Ministry which I found was like a prison where there was no freedom. I did not like the culture and structure of the Ministry in which I was a total misfit. I was almost suffocated to death. The Defence Ministry was created in order to establish civilian rule over the Armed Forces and in the process, a hybrid system was born. It is the Headquarters of the Army, Navy and Air Force who formulated and executed all Defence Plans, Programmes and proposals and the officers of the Ministry were expected to 'process' their proposals on a 'single file system'- the case files would come from and go back to the respective Headquarters. The proposals would be initiated by the Headquarters, processed and agreed to by the Ministry and transmitted back for implementation. The contribution of the Ministry was limited to offering comments on the proposals during processing and sometimes acting as a moderating influence. To me, the Defence Ministry appeared to be a redundant organization because all its functions could well be performed by the Army Navy and Air Force Headquarters. But there had been a deeper objective in the whole design - the Defence Ministry was the 'civilian face' of the Armed Forces, to act as a medium for interactions with the Parliament, the Central Ministries and the outside world. The idea was to insulate the Armed Forces from all social, political and economic forces sweeping the Nation and the World. But, what I disliked most was a constant pressure exerted on the ministry and the limited scope of using one's talent and decision-making power.

In this context, being a non-conformist myself, it was quite natural for me to seek an escape route to move out of the Ministry. The best opportunity I thought would be when I was to be picked up from the Deputy Secretary's panel for posting as Deputy Secretary. I made an appeal to the Administration for my placement in some other Ministry but the appeal was promptly rejected. Defence Ministry was a highly unpopular Ministry to the Organized Services, especially with the IAS officers who would always try to be accommodated in the Economic Ministries; for them, Defence Ministry would be the last preference because it could offer no 'perks', no facilities and no 'reward' but only slogging in high- tension jobs.

I was posted as Deputy Secretary in charge of Navy in rather tragic circumstances. One of the senior-most Deputy Secretaries, who was expected to take over as joint Secretary suddenly died of cardiac arrest. This officer who belonged to the Indian Railways was an officer of outstanding merit and efficiency. Perhaps, the habit of chain smoking snuffed off life of this bright officer. The situation I was placed in was grim, sombre and least desirable because of my fears of occupying the same chair but, there was no escape. My only worry was whether I would be able to match the reputation of my predecessor.

Since very few IAS officers were on offer (theoretically, there was no option, but there were ways of managing things not to join unpopular ministries), there were quite a few IAAS officers to manage the affairs of the Ministry. P. Krishnamurthy, Additional Secretary, K.R.Baliga, Joint Secretary, V. Srikantan, S, Laksminarayanan and T.S.Narasimhan, Deputy Secretaries, all belonged to Indian Audit & Accounts Service; I was the latest addition joining as a Deputy Secretary, thus having a dominant presence in all the major divisions of the Ministry. I would ask my self - what technical competence we all officers had to manage the vital affairs of defence? The dislike of the Armed Forces Headquarters for civilian officers of the Ministry was not entirely misplaced. But, then, the system made the civilian officers the 'linkmen', rather middlemen, to promote the interest of the Armed Forces. We were accepted as part of higher formation not always out of respect but for sheer self-interest. Soon after I took over charge, I had a bitter taste of the hostility of the uniformed people for not conforming to the accepted norms, however stupid those could be. One example of a faulty tradition, a rather dangerous practice which I tried to stop was terribly resented and I had to suffer humiliation. All officers of the Armed Forces are very fond of salutes - both receiving and giving. They are so used to the magic of salutes that some officers think that life is not worth living if he is not saluted wherever he goes. That had been a part of the military culture and perhaps there was nothing wrong with that culture which was oriented towards total discipline. But nothing in this world should be overstretched beyond a point when it starts violating the universal moral laws. There were well established rules in all three wings of the Armed Forces that all juniors should wish and salute, as part of showing respect to their seniors in and out of office even when they meet on the road or in the market but there was no specific instruction to salute when they are driving vehicles. This had been working well for decades. But the trouble started when somebody tried to tinker with the system. It happened like this.

A senior Navy officer along with his wife had gone out for an evening walk when some junior officers, whom he recognized, speeded past on their scooters without saluting him. Obviously, they did not do because the rules did not specifically provide for saluting from moving vehicles. But, this officer felt highly offended and insulted, more so because his wife was with him. Next day, the wounded officer shot out letters to the Headquarters asking them to change the existing rules and making it compulsory for the junior officers to salute their seniors even though they are on moving vehicles.

When there was a proposal to amend the existing instructions making it compulsory to salute, I strongly objected to this saying that it would be ridiculous and dangerous, to salute from moving vehicles, especially from two wheelers. The Headquarters do no relish any rejection of their proposals by the Ministry and would invariably make issues out of them and approach higher authorities for vindication of their stand. One day, the Defence Secretary, Sushital Banerjee, one of the most outstanding Defence Secretaries belonging to the first batch of IAS officers, called me and said that the Naval Chief had complained to him against my observations on the proposed instructions on saluting from moving vehicles was a 'perverted view' of military discipline and that they wanted that the amendments must be agreed to by the ministry. Mr. Banerjee added that he entirely agreed with my observations but there was a need to develop a special skill and sensitivity to deal with the Armed Forces. He showed extreme sympathy and sensitivity to my feelings asking me not to mind the harsh words they have used on the file. To ameliorate my wounded feelings further, he said he would himself deal with case and I need not bother about the matter at all. He also added that it was a very minor matter for the Ministry and did not concern any of the major policy issues; therefore, if the Chief wanted to amend certain instructions which concerned their internal disciplines, let the Chief have the pleasure of issuing it! Mr. Banerjee's soothing arguments brought considerable relief to my disturbed mind. Needless to say, the revised instructions making it compulsory to salute seniors from moving vehicles were issued.

The irony was the matter did not end there. Soon after I left the Ministry, my old colleagues told me that the instructions which I vehemently objected to had been withdrawn by all the three branches of the Armed Forces because a number of accidents, some fatal, had taken place while trying to salute senior officers from moving vehicles, particularly two wheelers and the practice caused considerable resentment among the ranks. The Armed Forces Headquarters did not have any alternative but to withdraw the instructions immediately. I had a big laugh; I only used common sense and universal morality. The common sense is, after all, so scarce in this world!

IX

A Reign of Terror

Except for the Gun Powder case of the fifties, till mid-seventies, people did not hear of any major corruption case in defence deals. This was because, like the Ministry of External Affairs, the Defence Ministry was on a different pedestal with a halo about it and the power and dignity it commanded, the President of India being the Supreme Commander of the Armed Forces. The Defence Ministry had always been headed by a senior national leader and statesman who could command respect from all quarters. It was unimaginable that Defence Ministers of such national standing would like any corrupt practice to sneak into this sensitive Ministry which is responsible for the security of the Indian Nation.

But the glorious chapter of the Ministry of Defence ended with the entry of a regional satrap and staunch Gandhi family loyalist as the Defence Minister. This had been as surprising as the removal of Sardar Swaran Singh and nobody expected it. The Defence Ministry had been chugging along merrily under the leadership of Mrs. Gandhi and all the functionaries- the chiefs of staff, Armed Forces Headquarters and officials of the Ministry were extremely happy in her regime; she was very quick and decisive in her decision making.

Moreover, all the Defence people felt proud that the Prime Minister was holding the Defence Portfolio. Nobody expected a change would take place so suddenly.

One day we were alerted that this regional leader was arriving at the Defence Ministry straight from the swearing in ceremony at Rashtraprati Bhawan on his appointment as Defence Minister. This was typical of Mrs. Gandhi's style of functioning; till the last moment, nobody would know what was in her mind and keeping others guessing, she would pull a surprise at the end. The real reasons which prompted her to appoint a regional leader not having any national standing as the Defence Minister were never known. The buzz on the corridors was that left to herself, she would never have entrusted a sensitive portfolio like Defence to a person like him but had to give in to the pressures of her son, then a rising star in Indian politics, who found him as a man of action and more importantly, totally subservient to him. Till the time Sardar Swaran Singh was in power, this young leader could not make much progress for his dream project which involved transfer of a vast tract of Defence land and was confident that the new Defence Minister would certainly go out of his way to fulfil his 'dream' and also take control of the Ministry. With the expansion and opening of the Defence Sector, realization came to many that they could strike gold in defence contracts and the easiest way of getting rich was to become Indian representative of some major defence manufacturers –an aspect he had an eye on.

The style of functioning of the state administration and state politicians in India is too well known. Therefore, when a regional leader is catapulted to the national level and that too, to the key Ministry of Defence which has an influence on our international relations, national and international defence strategies and national security, the result could be nothing but near disaster. This was the fear and it also happened exactly like this. An ill-equipped ad-hoc state administration was transplanted on the well-established top administration of the Defence Ministry which had its own age-old traditions, conventions, integrity and dignity. A horde of state officials who were close confidants to a former chief Minister with doubtful credentials and used to the feudal manners and style of functioning swarmed the Minister's office. All moral questions and conventions were thrown to the winds; we became helpless.

A reign of terror was unleashed by the new Defence Minister and his staff. We got a taste of the highhandedness and feudal moorings with which the new Defence Minister wanted to rule within a month when one of our colleagues, in the process of handling a parliament question, for no fault of his, was suspended by the Minister without any notice or warning. In some of the States in North India, the Chief Ministers who were semi-literate mainly ruled by 'suspensions', the only weapon and management technique they knew for controlling the bureaucrats in a complex administrative set-up. But, such a thing was unheard of in the Central Government, especially in the Central Secretariat. Till then, we never heard of any senior officer being suspended without notice in the Central Secretariat where only best officers were selected after a lengthy screening process. The question of suspension from the ministry job arose only when an officer was prima facie found, under the Conduct Rules, guilty of gross misconduct, corruption or dereliction of duty and a major punishment was proposed to be imposed for which an Inquiry Committee was required to be constituted. But the 'feudal lords' were not concerned with the rules or human rights! The incident shook us to the bones and all of us were so terrorized that every day, at the end of the day's work, we thanked God for not being suspended! Such a fear psychosis no Minister or not even a Prime Minister ever created in the Central Ministries; the relationship between the Minister and the senior officers had always been a relationship of mutual respect and not of hostility. In this difficult situation, we used to draw comforts by remembering more and more the days of Sardar Swaran Singh. Moreover, those were the days when a State of Emergency had been clamped on India by Mrs. Gandhi and during Emergency, most of the fundamental rights including the protection provided to the Civil Servants under the Constitution stood suspended. Therefore, even for minor lapses, one could lose his job and the prospect of being suspended and dismissed loomed large in the minds of all officials, high or low. The Emergency period had been the worst period in the lives of Indian bureaucrats destroying their morale and backbone till the Janata Government came to power when they tried to restore the confidence to work without fear or favour.

The personal staff of the Minister played havoc and they started indulging in all dubious practices, common in some state administrations but unheard of in Defence Ministry. Words started circulating in the Ministry that unless the Indian Agents of foreign firms visited the Minister's office and struck a separate "deal" with his Personal Staff, the pending contract files awaiting Minister's approval would not see the light of the day, however urgent the procurement proposals were. I could not believe it because all the proposals for procurement of weapons and military equipment and acquisitions of ships or aircraft carried secret or confidential tags and could be handled by only those who were authorized to deal with them. Secondly, it was beyond my comprehension that secret files containing matters of national security could be manipulated and misused to raise funds either for party or self in wanton violation of the oath taken by the Minister while assuming office. The personal staff could not have played the dangerous game without the consent of or at the behest of the Minister. I used to wonder why, again and again, the Minister's Personal staff enquired and asked for the various contract cases I had been dealing with. They kept a close eye on each and every contract which was under process in the Ministry and ensured that no contract slipped away from their watch-list.

X

Wiping Out Tears of an Air Marshall

I was not still fully convinced that such nefarious activities could be openly indulged in by the minister's office till I myself became a direct witness to the happenings. One day, a retired Air Marshall of the Indian Air Force (Air Marshal Ranjan Dutt) came to my room and broke down. He was almost inconsolable. I tried to bring him back to his normal self asking him to tell me the story and the truth before I could step in to help him out. Then he untwined his story. His wife had been suffering from breast cancer and he badly needed extra money as his pensions were not adequate to carry on the costly treatment. That's why he volunteered to act as the Indian Agent of a foreign firm although it was not a respectable job befitting his status. This firm had clinched a minor contract from which he was to receive a commission of 1 percent against the normal practice of 2-5 percent. The contract file had been cleared at all levels in the Headquarters and the Ministry but the personal secretary of the minister was firm on his parting with 50 percent of one per cent of the receivable commission. He did not know what to do next because without this money he would not be able to continue with the treatment of his beloved wife (I guess he married a foreign lady).

Nor did I know the way out. I thought for a while and it suddenly struck me that a Joint Secretary, a brilliant officer of the same State to which the Minister belonged and who recently joined as his main Adviser, could certainly help. This efficient and honest officer was, we were told, largely instrumental in the rise of this leader, once a small-time advocate in the district courts, and that he was so dependent on him that he would never say 'no' to this officer. So, it was a question of this officer's putting in a word to the Minister. I told Ranjan Dutt I did not personally know this officer except his reputation as a good man and suggested to him to seek an appointment with him and truthfully explain the whole matter. I was sure this Joint Secretary was kind-hearted enough to help him in his difficult times.

The trick worked. The day his contract file was cleared without "any damage", a beaming Ranjan Dutt entered my room will a smile and thanked me profusely.

I never felt so happy. At least, I could help somebody in his difficult time, who wanted to continue with the best possible medical treatment of his wife in critical conditions.

But the story of Air Marshal Ranjan Dutt also depressed me further and created real fears about my own safety and security and above all, my own clean image with the entire procurement of the Navy including acquisition and construction of ships, submarines and aircraft. The contracts were huge and the stakes very high. Ministers and their staff would come and go but the permanent civil servants who would remain would have faced the music. I was mortally afraid the misdeeds in the minister's office may land me in CBI and even in jail or I may lose my job. On the other hand, if the minister was unhappy with my obduracy, he could suspend me easily in those emergency days. This was the predicament and the great anguish with which we had to function. I was counting days for making an honourable exit from the Defence Ministry and go back to my parent Department where there was no tension or corruption nor political pressures.

But our sufferings ended rather abruptly. After one year of emergency rule, Mrs. Gandhi announced General Elections expecting to return to power with thumping majority, an assumption based on the achievements made during the emergency period. It is true that emergency corrected lot of distortions in the society - trains started running on time, the 'babus' started coming to office on time and work sincerely, bureaucrats became alert and responsive and public goods were delivered on expected lines. The economy also looked up and the growth rate doubled. But the excesses of the emergency like large scale arrest and detention without trial of the political opponents, gagging the press, force used in family planning campaign, demolition of slums and police excesses overshadowed the welcome changes and benefits of the emergency rule. Contrary to the predictions of her advisors and astrologers (they could not read the simmering discontent), Mrs. Gandhi and her Party, Congress (I) suffered a resounding defeat. It was the triumph of Jai Prakash Narain's movement for restoration of democracy. The Janata Government came to power and Morarjibhai Desai was elected the Prime Minister.

The Morarji Desai Government had been one of the best governments India had seen. It was transparent, efficient and people oriented. Most of the ministers being undisputed leaders of various political groups were stalwarts in their fields. For the bureaucrats, the period turned out to be a golden period. The Prime Minister asked all civil servants to be honest and work without any fear or favour. Instructions were issued from the Prime Minister's office that the civil servants should not obey verbal orders even if they came from the Minister. In case of emergent situations, the verbal orders may be acted upon but it must be immediately followed by confirmation in writing. It was strongly stressed that the civil servants' allegiance was to the Indian Constitution for which they have taken the oath and not to the individuals, be it the superior officer or the Minister. What could be more assuring and life-giving to the bureaucracy than this!

XI

Real Drama on the Aircraft Carrier

The Navy had a tradition of the Naval Fleet being reviewed periodically on sea usually on board the Aircraft carrier by the President of India, the Supreme commander of the Armed Forces. Being Deputy Secretary in charge of Navy, I was invited to this Ceremonial Parade conducted on board INS Vikrant. This is a grand spectacle with a large number of war-ships, submarines, fighter jets, helicopters, and other vessels demonstrating their weaponry and fire power in Blue waters. It is a life-time experience but I declined the offer because I was very sure that instead of a pleasure trip, I would land myself in a whirlpool of tension. I was particularly apprehensive of the most unpredictable behaviour and ruthlessness of the Minister. And surely, as I feared, the events which took place on INS Vikrant would put anybody to shame. The story goes like this.

To witness the Naval Review by the President, a large number of VVIPs and VIPs were invited to the formal ceremony on board INS Vikrant – Ministers, MPs, Secretaries and senior officers of the Armed Forces. Also invited was the Minister's guest, the young 'rising star of Indian politics' who was not holding any official position but wielded great power over the government. Strict protocol was to be observed for all ceremonies of the Armed Forces and for that matter all official ceremonies of the Government like the Republic Day Parade, the Independence Day function etc. and the seating arrangements are made in accordance with the warrant of precedent. Therefore, the seating arrangement on-board INS Vikrant was necessarily to be made in accordance with the Navy's long-standing tradition and therefore, this young rising politician, not holding any official position was seated amongst other VIPs. This enraged the Minister. He called the Chief of Naval Staff and insisted that his important guest should be seated next to the President, although his guest did not make any such demand. The Naval Chief explained to him that the Navy Protocol did not permit him to do so. The Minister was further infuriated and offered his own seat to his most important guest whom he considered more important than the President of India (for his personal political ambitions). The Minister reportedly told the Naval Chief, in the presence of all dignitaries 'I will suspend you'- the most potent weapon he had in his armoury.

The following day after the Naval Review was over, the corridors of South Block was abuzz with the news that the Navy Chief had met the Defence Secretary and submitted his resignation. We never found the Admiral, a nice gentleman, so agitated. Obviously, no Chief of Staff would tolerate such humiliation from the Minister made in public visibility. The Defence Secretary tried to persuade him to withdraw the letter and not to take such a drastic step but as the news filtered down, we came to know that he was adamant in his resolution to resign unless the Minster apologized to him.

This was an extremely dangerous game played by the Minister since this could have snow-balled into a major confrontation between the Armed Forces and the Civilian government striking at the very root of survival of democracy. It did not require much intelligence to understand that the supremacy of civilian control over the Armed Forces was exercised by the Defence Ministry by maintaining a delicate balance through amicable discussions and interventions at the highest levels. All Defence Ministers in the past had been extremely sensitive to this balance of power and had ensured that no discontent was allowed to breed and grow among the Armed Forces, particularly at the higher echelons of the Headquarters.

This delicate balance was violently disturbed in one crude incident on a non-issue. The Naval Chief's threat was almost a revolt against the civilian control.

Everybody in the Ministry understood its serious implications except perhaps by the Minister. It was quite certain that the Army chief and Air Force Chief would have joined in the fray had not the fire been stamped out quickly.

The matter went to Mrs. Gandhi who knew very well that such a thing never happened in the history of Independent India and also of the dangers of playing with fire. Mrs. Gandhi, a shrewd administrator, always kept an alternative reliable channel open through the Secretaries for receiving information about the happenings in various ministries. She used to have periodical meetings with the Secretaries who were encouraged to inform her on important developments taking place in their Departments. Mrs. Gandhi must have received information about this unfortunate episode and subsequent resignation threat of the Navy Chief. Within a span of 2-3 days, the Ministry was relieved to know that the matter had been amicably resolved and that the Admiral had withdrawn his letter of resignation.

Nobody knows that exactly transpired. It was reported that Mrs. Gandhi immediately called the Defence Minister and firmly told him not to tinker with the Armed Forces and to be extremely careful in dealing with the three Chiefs. Nobody knows whether the Minister apologized to the Chief of Naval Staff. After this, the Defence Minister never needled the Chiefs of Staff.

XII

Defence Secretaries - Different Hues

Four Defence Secretaries in four years! How can a uniform Defence Policy be followed with such frequent changes? The purpose of intensive training for the first two years given to the elite services at the National Academy of Administration had been not only to equip them well for their professions but also to iron out the angularities of officers coming from different backgrounds. A uniform style of functioning, a uniform pattern of behaviour with dignity and a minimum standard of efficiency in administration were expected of all officers when they occupied seats of power. It is doubtful if training can, except better knowledge inputs, dress code and table manners, improve very much the attitude to life, character and individual style of functioning. This is amply borne out by the fact that the four Defence Secretaries during my tenure had quite different approaches to problems and had quite contrasting behavioural attributes.

The first Defence Secretary I met was Govind Narain, a typical ICS officer of golden era - sophisticated, pleasant, and soft spoken, firm and decisive. He commanded respect from the juniors as well as the Ministers. His handling of politicians and the officers of the Ministry, whom he would take along with him, had been exemplary. He also earned full confidence of the Chiefs of Staff and other senior officers of the Armed Forces. All officers of the Ministry could expect to look to him as protector in moments of crisis. His style of functioning and his sharp intelligence, skill and empathy left no room for conflicts or controversies between the politicians and the bureaucracy and between the Ministry and the Armed Forces.

One small instance which I remembered vividly would reveal the capability, sharpness and intelligence of the man. The PAC headed by Jyotirmoy Basu selected an Audit Paragraph on a scandal in Ordnance Factories for oral evidence and summoned Defence Secretary along with the head of the organization. The Ministry was represented by the Additional Secretary, P. Krishnamurthy having an independent charge of Navy and Ordnance Factories, who led the delegation for oral evidence before the PAC. But the PAC did not agree to continue discussion with Krishnamurthy, adjourned the meeting and asked him to send the Defence Secretary next day. Immediately on his coming back, Krishnamurthy narrated his predicament to the Defence Secretary. Till then, Govind Narain knew nothing about the Audit Paragraph or of the scandal. He kept a briefing meeting in the afternoon with the concerned officers. During the meeting, heaps of documents and files and lengthy briefs were produced. Govind Narain did not wish to consult any of them and asked for the original copy of the Audit Report containing the Audit Paragraph. He read the Paragraph minutely and then asked a few questions by way of clarifications; he also asked the officers to tell him the truth and not to hide the lapses. While the officers were providing clarifications to his questions, Govind Narain jotted down a few points on his slip pad and dismissed the meeting shortly.

Next day, Govind Narain arrived at the PAC meeting for oral evidence and the only papers he carried with were his slip pad and the copy of the Audit Paragraph, something unheard of. He started by profusely apologizing for his inability to attend the meeting the previous day without making any reference to the incident that took place earlier. In his opening remarks revealing his oratorical skill, he eulogized the vast experiences of the members and politicians and how bureaucrats could learn and benefit from their experiences. Bureaucrats while trying to do their best, because of their limited vision and experience, do commit mistakes, sometimes unknowingly. He owned the lapses agreeing to all the observations of the CAG and promised that an enquiry would be held to bring the responsible officials to book and a report on the corrective action taken would be submitted to the PAC as early as possible. Thereafter, the Paragraph was hardly discussed and Govind Narain came back unscathed. Any other person in his place would have been in deep waters.

Govind Narain was succeeded by D.R. Kohli belonging the last generation of ICS officers. While he had been meticulous, his abrasive, rather arrogant style of functioning used to cause annoyance at all levels. As mentioned earlier, his handling of PAC was in sharp contrast with that of Govind Narain and a meeting which was scheduled for one day lasted for full two days and all his efforts caused further irritations resulting in a voluminous devastating report from the PAC. I also personally felt he was not a team man and sometimes his behaviour with senior officers bordered on verbal assaults.

Gian Prakash was the first IAS officer to become Defence Secretary, a senior and key post although there were still a few ICS officers left floating in the Central Secretariat, who would have, in the normal course, occupied the post. But many people attributed his rise to his closeness with Chaudhary Charan Singh. Raj Narain, the flamboyant politician was extremely critical of the officer, even telling in public that he neither saw 'gyan' nor 'prakash' in Gian Prakash. But that must been because of their past experiences with each other in UP.

Gian Prakash was a good man and trusted his officers fully, perhaps more than required. He was very quick to dispose of files and instead of wasting his time in wading through the files, he would generally agree with the wisdom of his senior officers whom he trusted.

Gian Prakash was soon elevated to the coveted post of Comptroller and Auditor General of India, a constitutional post equivalent to a Judge of the Supreme Court. Here again, in the race for appointment to the highest post available to the civil services of the country; he outsmarted his senior ICS officers. Two ICS officers – H.N. Ray, the serving Finance Secretary and M.M. Sen., Defence Production Secretary were the front runners and almost everybody thought that H.N. Ray would be the next Auditor General when Ardhendu Bakshi, an IA&AS officer demitted office. But to everybody's great surprise, Gian Prakash was appointed reportedly because of his high political connections. This is the first time that the post of Audit General was occupied by an IAS officer. Thereafter, the IAS officers had never loosened their grip on the coveted post and no IA&AS officer had been appointed as Auditor General even if history was on their side. The first few Auditor Generals after Independence belonged IA&AS and people like Narahari Rao, A.K. Chanda, A.K. Roy and Ardhendu Bakshi were stalwarts in their own rights as Auditor General.

Sushital Banerjee, a brilliant IAS officer, succeeded Gian Prakash. Sushital Banerjee who combined both head and heart was head and shoulder above other contemporary Secretaries with his immaculate behaviour, hard work, charm and sheer brilliance - brilliance radiating from with forehead with milk of kindness but firmness. I never felt so happy in my official life. You know there is somebody who will guide and will also protect you at all costs. I had many unforgettable experiences working with him, one of which is mentioned below. I had gone on to the Administrative Staff College, Hyderabad (ASCI) for MDP training. At the end of the programme, the participants were expected to submit a research paper. I wrote a paper on 'Decision-Making process at the Central Government' which was highly appreciated and subsequently. ASCI informed me that they wanted to publish the paper in their Journal, which they did. I received some encouraging response from various quarters; one of them was from an Agricultural University in Alaska.

Before the Article was published, I sent a copy to Sushital Banerjee for his perusal. Weeks passed. I thought being extremely busy, he would not have time to read it and the article must have been dumped somewhere in the heaps of unwanted papers. After about two months, the paper came back to me with a note complimenting me for the excellent effort and also saying that it had been an outstanding piece of work. I was surprised to see that he not only read the longish article in between the lines but also corrected at many places and offered his suggestions and comments for further improving certain portions of the paper. I was really touched. His compliments gave me enough energy and oxygen to sustain me well for the rest of my tenure in the Ministry.

It was a tragedy that untimely death cut short the brilliant career of this great civil servant, a genius, still down to earth. Sushital Banerjee's focus had always been the common man- the man at the Counters of the Post Office, the Railway Reservation office, the Banks, the Ration Shops, the Electricity office, the Telephone office and of the Municipalities. I heard him saying many a time that the government delivery systems should be oriented towards improving the functioning of these Counters the common people are concerned with. He was also a great votary of a Unified Civil Service which would have ended the bickering and rivalries of various civil services. According to him, a fresh UPSC Examination should be held for all officers reaching the level of Deputy Secretary in all Group 'A' Services and All India Services and the successful officers would be inducted into a united Civil Service to man the higher decision making posts (Joint Secretary and above) of the government. It will ensure that the most talented officers would be at the helm of affairs of running the administration of the country achieving greater efficiency by pooling the experiences in all disciplines.

Negotiating for months to get a fair deal for the country for the purchase and manufacture of Jaguar Fighter Aircraft, a multibillion dollar Project took a heavy toll on his health. He was visibly over- worked and over-burdened. In addition, he was asked to look after the vacant portfolio of Home Secretary. Working day and night at breakneck speed gave him a heart attack. He was admitted immediately to All India Institute of Medical Sciences (AIIMS). The doctors asked him not to do any work or even talk in ICU. But he pleaded with the doctors to allow him to see and finalize one case-file which was of vital importance to the Armed Forces – the new welfare measures for the entire personnel of the three Services- Army, Navy and Air Force. Sushital Banerjee, after examination and being satisfied with the proposal inked his signature on the file and the next moment, he dropped down dead. What a dramatic exit from this world!

XIII

Jagjivan Ram – the Premier Defence Minister

Like quick shuffling of Secretaries, shuffling of Ministers had been the order of the day. During a span of four years, we had to face four Defence Secretaries as well as four Defence Ministers – Sardar Swaran Singh, Indira Gandhi, Bansi Lal and Babu Jagjivan Ram.

Jagjivan Ram had been the oldest and most experienced of all the Ministers in the Union Cabinet and a constant factor since the pre-Independence Interim Government till his death. He had been a Cabinet Minister in the Cabinet of all Prime Ministers spanning over 40 years till 1980s and had the experience of handling almost all the major Ministries of Government of India under various Congress and non-Congress regimes. He became the Defence Minister during the Janata regime by switching over his loyalty from Congress to the other side (which was reversed on the fall of Janata Government) retaining a separate identity for his group. There was hardly any politician on the Indian scene that time, who could match his intelligence, shrewdness, efficiency and coolness. As Defence Minister, he had been simply outstanding and had certainly been one of the most successful, if not the best, Defence Ministers. While he might look at first sight somewhat unimpressive to many, his poise, personality, knowledge, decision-making ability, wisdom and command over language earned him the loyalty of everybody- the Service Chiefs, Secretaries and other functionaries of the Ministry. He was a team man and had built an unassailable team around him, who would give their best for him. Everybody was happy with him with his soft spoken, firm and affectionate manners (nobody had seen him speaking raising his voice even in moments of anger). We knew he was a hard task master but also a protector. He could do nothing wrong.

Jagjivan Ram had an astonishing power of taking a balanced decision in a worst situation. He had developed a system of his own which activated the decision-making process to move faster contrary to the traditional Secretariat system which was oriented to file pushing from the bottom. As for example, he introduced a system of weekly briefings with the three Chiefs, Defence Secretaries and other senior officers of the Ministry, supposed to be an informal meeting, but assumed the importance of formal conference as it reviewed the defence preparedness on continuing basis and propelled the Ministry and the Headquarters to initiate advance actions. Through methods like this, Jagjivan Ram established his grip and control over the affairs, a rare phenomenon is the Indian system of governance.

One small incident which occurred in Parliament and which I vividly remember demonstrated the spark of brilliance of this man. I was in the official gallery to assist the Minister of State in answering a *starred question* on submarine projects. Not satisfied with the written reply, a volley of inconvenient questions was raised by the Opposition, which the Minister could hardly reply satisfactorily. There was near pandemonium and the situation was getting out of control. Jagjivan Ram who was listening to the debate slowly rose and gave a spell-binding 5-minute speech even though he had no briefings and hardly knew about the question. He spoke of the security situation around us and how vital the submarine project was for the security of the country and how discussion of such secret defence projects in the open forum like the Parliament could seriously compromise the security of the nation and how our hostile neighbours and enemies would benefit from such a discussion. He did not touch the subject matter of the question at all but such had been his convincing power that there was pin-drop silence in Parliament. No further question was asked on the issue.

Jagjivan Ram, a great son of India, had already become a legend during his life time. It was a tragedy for the country that political machinations prevented Jagjivan Ram from becoming the first Dalit Prime Minister of India. Following the breakup of the Janata Coalition, he had the best opportunity of being appointed as the Prime Minister. He wanted only two weeks' time from the President, Sanjeeva Reddy to muster enough support from the other political parties. It was believed that had he got this much of time from the President, he would have definitely received the support of a large number of Dalit and other MPs to enable him to form the Government. The President, supposedly under the pressure of the Congress Party, did not oblige him.

A great opportunity for better governance of the country was lost. Had Jagjivan Ram been made the Prime Minister, the history of the country would have been different and certainly for the better. With his great administrative skill, unmatched experience and efficiency, we were certain the country could have been on the road of rapid progress and development. But that was not fated to be. General Elections were called and Mrs. Gandhi came back to power again. An era of political turbulence, 'Operation Blue Star' and finally her assassination by her own bodyguards brought the country to a near- chaotic situation.

XIV

Fight Wars and Lose Promotion!

An unusual but a very poignant letter addressed to the Defence Minister, Jagjivan Ram was received in the Defence Ministry from a retired Principal of a school in North Bengal who wrote about the denial of promotion to his son, a Major in the Army. The letter was significant because it raised the fundamental question of criteria for promotion to higher places in the

Armed Forces - is it for fighting wars for the country or for socialization and sycophancy?

This particular Major had been a brilliant student having topped the Matriculation Examination in the whole district. His father, a Headmaster in East Bengal had to flee from his native village along with his family, relatives and Hindu neighbours leaving everything behind to save themselves from the murderous Muslim mobs. They travelled for two days without food and water secretly through the jungle and river routes and reached the Indian borders of Jalpaiguri where they lived as refugees. His father, because of his qualifications and experience as Headmaster got a job as Principal in a school in Jalpaiguri. When his son stood first in the district, the District Magistrate visited his house to congratulate him and he became instrumental, offering all possible help to him including scholarships, for NDA Examination and his final selection as an Army Officer. He joined the Army against all opposition from his family and friends.

This Major was a quiet type; spoke very little, never smoked, never drank, never socialized and was a workaholic full of idealism and patriotism. He did not know how to keep his bosses and their wives pleased. But, he fought two great wars with all the bravery and sincerity available at his command. In the Sino- Indian War 1962, as a Captain in the Signals, he was in the forefront in the NEFA region where his unit was attacked by the Chinese. The entire company was wiped out; only three people including him miraculously escaped. They strayed into the jungles and got lost. For about a month, they travelled through the forests without knowing the correct directions and the escape routes. They survived on leaves, fruits and roots and rested on the trees for the nights. After about a month, an Army rescue team spotted him and picked him up in a disoriented state and admitted to an Army Hospital. He could not remember what happened to him and what the fate of his other two colleagues was. He was suffering from serious diarrhoea, dehydration and malnutrition. It took months to bring him back to near normal health and he was subsequently allowed to go home and also rejoin the Army after mandatory de-briefing because it was suspected that he must have been captured and later released by the Chinese. But, the end result was he was medically downgraded and lost his next promotion.

Meanwhile, his family especially his beautiful young wife to whom he was married only a few months before the war and his old father had a harrowing time spending sleepless nights. One day, an Army wire (telegram) reached them saying that the "Captain was reported missing". He had been the main bread earner in the family and the education and future career of his brothers and sisters entirely depended on his income (one brother was in a medical college and another brother was doing engineering). There was no information about him for a month and the family was slowly reconciling with the obvious conclusion that he must not have been alive and was therefore, thinking of the last rights to be performed. Suddenly, an Army messenger landed at their house and broke the news that the Captain was recovering in an Army Hospital somewhere in Assam. Think of the waves of joy, disbelief and relief which his young wife and the entire family got at that moment. His father along with the daughter in law rushed to Assam and the Major was reunited with his wife who took care of him after his discharge. But the Army bureaucracy did not give any credit for his miraculous escape and survival and he lost his promotion.

During the Bangladesh Liberation War 1971, as Army Major, he played an extraordinarily exemplary role. Being a Bengali, he was assigned the task of training *Mukti Bahini* (the Liberation Force) soldiers and mobilising them on the Indo-Bangladesh borders. As it is well known, the *Mukti Bahini* fought Pakistani soldiers alongside the Indian Army and because of their full knowledge of the terrain, guided the Indian Army in all strategic encounters. This Major entered Bangladesh along with the *Mukti Bahini* from the Tripura borders and was in the first group to land in the capital Dacca. When Dacca was captured and brought under the control of the Indian Army, he was made the

Adjutant being a common link between the Army, the *Mukti Bahini* and the local administration. In spite of his great contribution to Bangladesh's freedom struggle, one brutally honest act of his which went against his superior's utterly corrupt intentions was sufficient to bring him in the bad books of selfish superiors. The Commanding officer of the Dacca Region, a Major General asked him to ensure safe passage of a truck containing highly valuable goods and prized seizes collected during the raids. When 91,000 Pakistani Army personnel surrendered to the Indian Army authorities, the top brass of the Pakistani Army had to vacate their official residences leaving everything behind. The valuable items which included gold and jewellery, artefacts, designer furniture and wardrobe, Persian carpets, electronic gadgets etc. were seized as war trophies. One Major-General who collected lot of these trophies (spoils of the looting) got them packed in an Army truck and ordered this Major to transport to India. The major knowing its contents flatly refused to do so and advised the Major General not to indulge in this misadventure because the *Mukti Bahini* people were everywhere and if they had any inkling of the idea, it will not only be big scandal for the Indian Army but also for India and it would also be end of their careers. The Major General understood and realising his folly asked for his advice. The Major told him 'if you trust me, leave the matter to my discretion, I shall do the needful'. What the Major did was something extraordinary. At the dead of night, he took the truck with a few helpers to river Meghna (which is so big that the other shore cannot be seen) and asked his Jawans to throw down each and every article into the Meghna to be washed away into the sea and in the process washed away all the sins of the Indian Army. The story never came out in the public. But secret reports of the Army intelligence put question marks on various acts of commission and omissions on the part of the senior Army Officers during the military campaign in Bangladesh. The Commanding Officer of the Eastern Region who was responsible for the Bangladesh Operations was also ignored from being considered as the Chief of Army Staff, perhaps because of serious veiled allegations about integrity.

Needless to say, this Major got a bad chit from his immediate superior whose war trophies were all offered to the river Meghna and lost his promotion although he was one of the crazy characters who won a glorious war in Bangladesh against a wily and formidable enemy Pakistan.

The retired Principal went on to say that he was not writing the letter because of his own son having been ignored but for all others who have fought wars but lost their promotions because of their inability to compromise with unethical materiality. The majority of officers who have made it to the top have not fought wars or made any sacrifice but their perfect inter-personal relationships propelled them to the ever higher levels. The Defence Ministry should have a deeper introspection on the basic criteria of elevating people to the higher ranks – professional capabilities and achievements or personal achievements?

The Defence Minister was sad to read the letter and asked the Army Headquarters to review his case. Nothing was heard after that; obviously, the Army bureaucracy did not allow any such review in a serious manner. So the officer retired as Major in the time-scale of Lt. Colonel in spite of fighting two great wars for India.

XV

A Peep into the Past – My Bhopal Days

The manner in which I landed in the Ministry of Defence, initially as under Secretary and then as Deputy Secretary had been rather ironic. I had no expertise or experience or inclination, which could serve as a criterion for my selection. I was one of the victims of usual egotist wars. I belonged to the Indian Audit and Accounts Service, considered to be an elite Service those days, which I had elected for against all other services. I was quite happy at Bhopal working as Dy. Accountant General (Works), an independent charge, looking after the auditing and reporting functions of all the Engineering Divisions of Madhya Pradesh State –Public Works, Irrigation, River valley Projects and Public Health Engineering Departments. When I was transferred from Calcutta to Bhopal is early 1971, I was little scared, but I was told by New Delhi that it was a honeymoon posting for me (since I was just married) which turned out to be true. The four years we spent at Bhopal had been delightful years full of excitement, charm and indolence. The ability to move freely among the *Nawabs* and *Begums* of the old princely state, the politicians and bureaucrats of the new capital with a small size population gave a great deal of satisfaction and meaning to life. I became a part of the cultural circles of Bhopal. I remember I played the leading role in a play (Rithwik Ghatak's 'Meghe Dhaka Tara') staged during Durga Puja, which was directed by the famous journalist writer Tarun Kumar Bhaduri (Jaya Bachchan's father). We were regular visitors to Tarunda's place and we witnessed with amazing interest Jaya Bhaduri's gradual blossoming into an accomplished action leading to her marriage with Amitav Bachchan.

Initially, I was short-listed for a position of Under Secretary in the Department of Economic Affairs (DEA) considering my background in Economics as a student and a college Lecturer. But, the orders never came. The then Comptroller And Auditor General of India (CAG), the cadre controlling authority, felt he could not be taken for granted since his prior consent was not taken before my selection by DEA. Many months later, I received on order from CAG posting me to the Ministry of Defence as Under Secretary. The order was rather peculiar in that it contained a chain of cross-country posting and I was the last in the chain. I could see that there was no chance of my getting relieved from my present post in the next six months. I received a call from the Accountant General, Mr. Ramachandran, a fine human being, who had been my immediate boss, saying that I should start packing up my establishment and take up the new assignment within a month's time. He himself missed a chance of going to the Central Secretariat in similar circumstances and he did not want, out of his of profuse affection for me that the same thing should happen to me. Therefore, he decided to relieve me by the end of the month and inform the headquarters. But this was not to happen. Promptly, a reply came from the CAG that AG should have been mindful of the spirit of the order and that the chain of posting should be strictly followed. Mr. Ramachandran was highly apologetic and told me during his next visit to Bhopal 'Brahma, I have no face to show it to you'. Being a junior officer, this embarrassed me a great deal. I quietly cancelled the tickets and waited indefinitely for my relief order. Meanwhile, there had been a spate of farewell dinners some of which had been postponed. This was the second time that such a thing happened to me in Bhopal. The first time it happened within six months of my posting to Bhopal. I suddenly received an order transferring me to Wellington to undergo a one-year course in National Defence College. Since I was newly married and enjoyed the hospitality of Bhopal, I was in no mood to face another transfer. With the assistance of my AG at Gwalior, this order was finally cancelled. But we had already attended a number of dinner parties organized to bid us farewell.

It took me nearly six months to get relieved from Bhopal to join the Ministry of Defence, New Delhi. During the intervening periods a series of misfortunes occurred. My wife had been at an advanced stage of pregnancy and had to be sent out to Calcutta. I could accompany her only up to Jabalpur to put her into Bombay Mail. I put her in a first class compartment and requested the co-passengers to help her if she needed any till her journey to Howrah station. It was almost a criminal neglect on my part to allow her to leave alone in the first class compartment from Jabalpur to Calcutta. One my return to Bhopal from Jabalpur, after a few days, I was running very high temperature and there was nobody to look after me in the house which after my wife's departure, almost became a haunted place for me. This was a big house with 30 rooms, courtyard and garden belonging to an aristocrat Muslim who migrated to Pakistan and on its automatic transfer to the state, it was allotted on permanent basis to the Accountant General, MP for the residence of the Deputy AG. The entire area known as Ameerganj had been an aristocratic area where still lived a number of *Chhota Nawabs* and *Begums* and some loyalists belonging to the old Bhopal state. In fact, my immediate neighbours were Dr. Khan related to the Bhopal royal family and the Nawab of Muhammadgarh, a tiny princely state near Bhopal, practically a Zamindar. It was a nightmarish experience to live in this fort-like house. Obviously, I spent many sleepless nights. One great advantage, against all odds, had been that my office was less than 5 minutes walk from my residence and I could always ask my officers to come with the files and dispose them of in royal style. My office was located in one portion of Tajmahal Building, the seat of power of the Bhopal Begums. It was believed that the royal family got a curse not to have a male heir or Nawab. There was another story that all the Nawabs of Bhopal who tried to complete 'Taj-ul-Masajid', the grand mosque opposite Tajmahal Palace and designed to be bigger than the Jama Masjid of Delhi, died young the last one leaving no male heir. Thereafter, a succession of Begums ruled the Bhopal State till its integration to Madhya Pradesh State. After integration, the Begums' headquarters, Tajmahal Building, a huge *bulbulaiya* type of structure was occupied by the Sindhi refugees and only a small portion could be saved to house the AG's office. It again became a haunted place and I never ventured to cross over to the other side.

My fever did not subside for five days. Knowing that I was too ill to go to office, Dr. Bose dropped in to examine me. Dr. Bose had been the Chief Civil Surgeon of the Bhopal State and personal physician to the Royal family. He was a legendary figure in Madhya Pradesh and was regarded as a God-like personality with unblemished reputation and a phenomenal capacity for correct diagnosis. I got the proof immediately. He told me he was suspecting malaria but I could not believe saying that malaria had been totally eradiated in the country and I had not heard any case of malaria in Calcutta, Madhya Pradesh or elsewhere. In fact, malaria medicines were off the shelves of the chemist shops and the doctors had forgotten the prescription for treatment of malaria. Dr. Bose did not say anything, asked me to dress up and took me in his car to Hamidia Hospital for a simple blood test.

In the evening, Dr. Bose confirmed the blood sample did indeed show presence of malaria parasites. Fortunately, the prescribed dose of medicines which were out of market was available with him, which he sent down asking me to scrupulously follow the instructions for taking those medicines. Mrs. Bose went on sending fresh fruit juice, soup and boiled vegetables for 3 days. My indebtedness to Bose family went on mounting and I did not know how to repay at least at portion of this debt in my life time.

My fever had gone on the 3rd day after starting the bitter medicines and went to office on the fourth day when news came that my wife had delivered our first baby, a boy, by caesarean section. I was little worried because this had been her third operation on the abdomen; her appendicitis operation at Bhopal earlier led to serious infections and it took three months for her to recover. Next day, I got the news that my co-brother (my wife's eldest sister's husband) suddenly died in a nursing home at Chandannagar near Calcutta out of uncontrolled bleeding from the stomach. My wife had not been told about this tragedy and she was singularly unaware of what was happening around her. What would be her reaction if she was told the tragedy occurred on the same day when her son was born? Her wounds were yet to heal. In these circumstances, I had no option but to rush to Calcutta. It was not easy to reach Calcutta from Bhopal – it would take about 40 hours by train, first by Bilaspur Express to Jabalpur and then by Bombay Mail from Jabalpur via Allahabad. It was also not easy to get train reservations to and fro at short notice.

I became almost a mental wreck. Again, Dr. Bose gave me all the courage and advice. With the help of the Area Railway Manager, all the tickets and reservations were tied up. I decided to go without waiting for a formal sanction of leave. I wrote a letter to the AG explaining the circumstances and also saying that I had a nervous breakdown and that I needed at least for 10 days' leave (I should have mentioned that autocracy of the Headquarters office was responsible for this but could not mention out of fear of reprisal). On reaching Howrah, I went straightway to my wife's parental place at New Barrackpore, another two hours journey from Howrah station. I forgot all my worries and troubles when I saw our son (our only child), very fair, smiling and not troubling his mother at all. I looked after my wife and child for ten days and prepared to return to Bhopal, again through a tortuous journey by train.

Coming back to Bhopal, I was told by my AG, R.N. Joshi, an exceedingly pleasant and friendly person, my troubles were going to be over and that he was making some special arrangements, by using his influence in the Headquarters wherefrom he was posted to Gwalior, to relieve me early.

I started packing. But there was hardly anything requiring packing. All the furniture in the house was rented from state PWD. Therefore, except our clothing, crockery, utensils and small personal items, there was nothing to pack. Still, trunks and suitcases and other materials made a good number of 20 packages, which I intended to carry with me in my first class compartment.

I was finally relieved of my post on 10th November 1974 by local arrangement by sending an officer from Gwalior on temporary transfer to Bhopal. This could have been six months back, which could have avoided humiliating my AG and causing untold miseries to me. That was how the Headquarters office was attuned to function at that time - obviously without a human face.

And what happened to the much flaunted long chain of cross country posting orders? It could not be implemented fully because somebody in the middle broke the chain using his influence and clout.

This time, except with Dr. Bose and one or two close families, I avoided accepting lunches and dinners. I was almost in a state of mental wreck and life appeared depressive with the prospect of an uncertain future in Delhi without my family, without a house, without transport, without friends and without any domestic help. My depression led to so much of negativism that I did not feel like attending even the reception hosted by Tarunda to celebrate Jaya's wedding with Amitav Bachchan. There was of course another sentimental reason that Tarunda being so close to us did not personally come or even ring up asking us to come for the reception and sent the invitation card by post. Today, people would die to get an invitation for such occasions. We never met Jaya and Tarunda after this – Tarunda died in Bhopal after a few years and Jaya became out of bounds.

I decided to leave Bhopal for Delhi on 12th November by G.T. Express which had a stoppage of just five minutes at Bhopal Station. I was overwhelmed to see that at least one hundred officers and staff came to the station to see me off. When the train arrived, my entire luggage was put inside in no time, which almost filled the whole compartment to the annoyance of the follow passenger. But he was mollified after my officers pleaded with him saying that their Sahib was going to Delhi on transfer to join a Central Ministry. From an easy life to the unknown, I did not know how to set up a home at Delhi. I had a friend from my Hyderabad days, a bachelor who shared an accommodation with another bachelor at Hauz Khas, South Delhi. I wrote to him about my adventure of carrying everything with me on GT express arriving New Delhi in the early morning of 13th November. I only hoped he would come to the station to rescue me! He did not disappoint me.

One of the pleasant memories I carried of the last few days of Bhopal had been an unexpected visit of Begum of Muhammadgarh, a stunningly beautiful lady in her early forties to my residence a day before I left Bhopal to say good-bye.

It was such a surprise for me particularly when the neighbourhood knew that my wife had left for Calcutta a few months back and I was staying alone in the bungalow. She came with another lady of the locality, a friend of my wife, to express her sympathies for the tragedy in the family and also to congratulate us for being blessed with a son. The Begum spent an hour and during the entire conversation, I could notice she was an epitome of grace and charm. It is still a mystery to me why the Begum chose to come down to my place to say good bye. Later on, I could realize that the Begum perhaps having lost a son saw an image of her son in me in my younger days.

Chapter Two

Civil Aviation Not Taking Off

I

Open Sky Policy

The Air Corporations Act, 1953 converted the vast Indian sky into a bonded sky. The Act created two monopoly Corporations - Indian Airlines (IAC) for domestic operations and Air India (AI) for international operations. By one stroke, the entire airline industry in India was nationalized. Seven domestic airlines – Deccan Airways, Airways India, Bharat Airways, Himalayan Aviation, Kalinga Airlines, Indian National Airways and Air Services of India were merged to form the state-owned new domestic airline. Indian Airlines Corporation inherited a fleet of 99 aircraft - 74 Dakotas, 12 Vikings, 3 DC-4s and various smaller types from the seven acquired airlines. After the creation of Indian Airlines, no other Indian or foreign airlines were allowed to be registered and operate on the domestic routes except occasional chartered flights.

Similarly, the same Act created Air India by nationalizing Air India International controlled by the Tatas. Air India was founded by J.R.D.Tata in July 1932 as Tata Airlines, a division of Tata Sons Ltd. (now Tata Group). On 15 October 1932, J. R. D. Tata flew a single-engine De Havilland Puss Moth carrying air mail (postal mail of Imperial Airways) from Karachi to Ahmedabad and Bombay (Juhu Airstrip). Royal Air Force pilot, Neville Vincent took the same aircraft continuing its journey to Madras via Bellary. Tata Airlines became a public limited company on 29 July 1946 under the name Air India. In 1948, after the Independence, 49% of the airline was acquired by the Government of India, with an option to purchase an additional 2%. In return, the airline was granted status to operate international services from India as the designated National Carrier under the name *Air India International*. The inaugural flight of Air India took place on 8th June 1948 when *Malabar Princess* (a Lockheed Constellation L-749) took off from Bombay for London via Cairo and Geneva. This marked the airline's first long-haul international flight; this was followed by services to Nairobi via Aden in 1950.

On 1st August 1953, the Government of India exercised its option to purchase a majority stake in the carrier and Air India International Limited was born as one of the fruits of the Air Corporations Act that nationalized the air transportation industry. At the same time all domestic services were transferred to Indian Airlines. In 1954, the airline took delivery of its first L-1049 Super Constellations and started services to Bangkok, Hongkong, Singapore and Tokyo.

Air India International entered the Jet Age in 1960 when it acquired its first Boeing aircraft (707-420), which was named as *Gauri Shankar*. In the same year, Jet services to London and New York were inaugurated on 14 May 1960. On 8 June 1962, the airline was officially renamed as Air India. On 11 June 1962, Air India became the world's first all-jet airline.

The Act could not, of course, prohibit international airlines from operating in Indian skies since under International Law, the member countries cannot deny access to Indian destinations on the international air routes. International operations into and out of India were governed by the modalities of bilateral air services agreements signed between India and other nations, under which the designated national carriers could operate a fixed number of flights to the designated destinations. The only exception had been the USA which had, because of historical reasons and being the number one world power, the right of operating unlimited number of flights by their civil carriers to friendly countries including India while all other countries were subjected to bilateral agreements even with the United States.

The circle was complete in 1993, exactly after 20 years, when the Air Corporations Act, 1953 was repealed ushering in an era of 'Open Sky Policy'. This was a bold step and a significant step taken by the Narasimha Rao Government towards liberalization. The Act was scrapped with the objective of generating healthy competition and growth of air transportation services by allowing private airlines to compete not only with Indian Airlines but also with themselves. It was expected competition would lead to substantial reduction in airfare and lower regime of tariff would lead to quantum jump in air traffic. The purpose was not to de-nationalize Air India or Indian Airlines but to free the air services sector from the stranglehold of the two monopolies known for their monumental inefficiency and elitist culture, reduce cost of air journeys making it affordable to the common man and also to give a boost to all the industries associated with the air transportation services.

II

Air India: Never Taking Off!

In the 1960s, Air India became the first all-jet airline in the world, a pioneer and a leader in international air services. But the airline suffered from stagnation with an average fleet of 26 aircraft, mostly obsolete, for almost five decades. Complacency made them oblivious of the need for modernization to face increasing competition in the international market. In sharp contrast, Singapore Airlines started with two old aircraft and two pilots borrowed from Air India and requested Air India to help them build an air line from scratch proving all technical assistance. Within a span of two decades, Singapore Airline became a giant airline with more than 100 aircraft with a most modern fleet while Air India was gradually reduced to a minor airline with hardly any significant share in international traffic from a position of a major and pioneer air line. While other major airlines like Singapore Airlines had been operating with an average of less than 100 persons per aircraft, Air-India's average touched almost 1000 personnel per aircraft. Clearly, this had been too unsustainable a situation for any airline.

On top of this, the wage bill started soaring. By 1995, within a period of 5 years, Air India's wage bill increased three fold to almost Rs.900 crore which caused operating losses. A survey conducted by me of the wage structures of the major foreign airlines showed that pilots of Air India were the highest paid in the world, much more than what was being paid by British Airways, Delta, United Airlines, Air France or Lufthansa. In 1995, the tax-free income of a Commander (Captain) of Air India averaged a whopping Rs. 60 lakh a year or Rs. 5 lakh per month. Unbelievable, if you consider the purchasing power parity. There were almost three dozen heads or categories under which pay and allowances of pilots were paid. In addition, the Company provided them housing accommodation, free medical and transport services. The Income Tax Authorities constantly tried to bring them under the tax net but every time they failed as the powerful Pilots Guild obtained stay orders from the courts and the Company had to bear the tax liabilities of the pilots from the Company's account. Some of the pilots, those who were detailed for duties of VVIP flights had established close connections with the Prime Minister's office and even the President's office and the management were helpless to take any action against the pilots. The pilots did not know how to spend their money. Some of them had, therefore, purchased houses in London, New York or Sydney and sent their sons and daughters to USA, UK or Australia for higher studies. They were the real Maharaja of Air India!

For this, the government of the day was solely responsible. Right from the days of Nehru, no government had made any serious effort to professionalize the organization. The Air India Board was hardly constituted on professional basis - it was stuffed with favourites, an important source of government patronage. The Managing Director had always been a bureaucrat, normally an IAS officer of the rank of Joint Secretary chosen, not on merit, but among those who had a political clout or enjoyed the confidence of the Civil Aviation Minister and the Prime Minister's Office. The result of the political-bureaucrat nexus had been disastrous for Air India. The Minister tended to be the undisputed Nawab and the MD the Zaminder of the vast Estate called Air India.

During my tenure, there was one attempt to infuse professionalism by reconstituting the Air India and Indian Board s into a common Board and making Russy Modi, one of the most successful MDs of TISCO the Chairman of both the Airlines. Here again, the measure was only half-hearted. The common Chairman was made a non-executive Chairman and two IAS officers were made MDs of Air India and Indian Airlines. While the Board consisted of a few experts like Deepak Parikh, it was overwhelmingly packed with people who had no knowledge or connection with the airlines industry like an MD of a gramophone company, the proprietor of a 'paan massala' company and the proprietor of a plantation enterprise. Therefore, it was always the official position, rather the Ministry's position which always prevailed.

Russy Modi soon discovered he was powerless. He also discovered that the Boards of which he was the common Chairman were dummy Boards having practically no power of effective decision-making. The Boards had no power to take final decisions on investments, acquisition of aircraft, choice of fleet, expansion of fleet, external borrowings, restructuring and even on internal affairs like crackdown on striking employees. Both inside and outside the Board room, Russy Mody would express his disappointment and helplessness for not being able to do anything for the Airlines. During an interview with a correspondent, which was published in India Today, Mody made an unguarded comment that he could not take orders from 500-odd MPs to run the airline. Perhaps, he told the truth and his statement was too straight forward and too blunt. There was uproar in Parliament and he was summoned to tender his apology and withdraw his comments, which he did. Not satisfied with this, he was humiliated and was asked to leave the House. He was forced to admit that, Air India existed and thrived because of the support of the Parliament and not in spite of it!

After this incident, the talkative Russy Mody went into recluse and hardly talked to anybody and shut his door for the Press people. During his entire tenure Russy Mody could not move an inch towards improving the efficiency of the Airlines and they remained where they were before he took over. Not only this, both the Airlines were facing financial disaster because for the first time, they started making operating losses. Needless to say, Russy Mody, the icon of the private sector success story, left Air India in utter disgust.

In sharp contrast, the management Board of Singapore Airline (which was largely controlled by the government) was given full autonomy and full powers to take commercial decisions concerning the business of the airline. I remember a few Directors going to the Paris Air Show in France and taking an on the spot decision to acquire half a dozen latest version aircraft assessing their technological superiority and better fuel efficiency. It took only two weeks for them to place an order with the manufacturer. It would have taken at two years if Air India wanted to place similar orders for their fleet.

In 1995, Air India wanted to add two aircraft to its existing fleet of 747-400 LR (Jumbo Jet) for long-haul operations exercising their option under the same contract and at the same price. But, it took exactly two years to procure these two aircraft. The process of acquisition of aircraft, even a single aircraft (which of course were very cost-intensive, sometimes costing Rs.700 crore per aircraft) involved approval by the full Board after technical and financial evaluations were complete, the Pre-PIB, the Planning Commission, the Ministry of Finance, the PIB (Public Investment Board) and finally the Cabinet. The same procedure applied to all Central Public Sector Undertakings. I thought, perhaps no country in the world had such a fool-proof, strict and dilatory system.

The abuse and misuse of Air India and Indian Airlines were almost limitless. Both the employees and the employers exploited the airlines to the lees. The pilots, air hostesses and the stewards were the most privileged, more privileged than their counterparts in any other airline of the world, in terms of hefty tax-free income, housing, transport, medical facilities, leave, duty period, food, number of free passes including life-long passes and other freebies. It was unthinkable that a full lunch cost only Re.1 for the all airline staff (in 1995) when the cost of a coca-cola was more than one rupee! All efforts by the Board to recover the service cost or at least a part of it met with stiff resistance, even threats of a strike. Such was the belligerency of the Unions! So, all the MDs except Air Marshall P. C. Lal followed an appeasement policy. The Unions of both the Airlines claimed the heads of many MDs including P. C. Lal.

Abuse and misuse of Air India like up-gradations, issue of free tickets, free entertainment and hotel accommodation and costly gifts including supply of foreign liquor had been a daily affair. But what shocked many including the Press and me were certain extreme misuses shamelessly perpetrated by the men in power.

A Managing Director of Air- India made a sojourn to Europe with his entire family (of course accommodated in First Class), visited a number of cities for two weeks, had a ride in the newly opened

Tunnel Train from London to Paris, hired a helicopter to go to Monte Carlo and Casablanca and all costs were borne by Air India. The same MD had kept two official accommodation s –one at Bombay and another at Delhi. He would an average of two weeks in Delhi, stay in his own house but claim daily allowance at hotel rates. He also got a letter written from the Ministry to the Estate Office that for the house he retained in Delhi, the market rent would be borne by Air India. It was discovered later that such a letter had never been by the Ministry. These were high -level white-collar crimes, for which CBI filed charge-sheets against the officer. But the irony was the then Secretary, Personnel who belonged to the same Cadre dropped the cases one by one and the indicted officer was promoted to higher levels and even reached the highest level of bureaucracy.

A Minister of Civil Aviation was advised a minor surgery (hernia), which could have been well performed at All India Institute of Medical Sciences, Delhi or in Jaslok Hospital, Bombay decides to go to London for the surgery. He stayed at St. James Court, a five star hotel for more than a month and all costs of surgery and recovery at the hotel were paid for by Air India. Most probably, the suggestion to get the surgery done at London came from the bureaucrat MD who made the Minister his life- long benefactor.

Air India had been made responsible for Haj Operations every year involving nearly a lakh of passengers. While accepting financial benefits for Haj pilgrimage was itself against the Shariat, which had been pointed out by many Muslim scholars, Government of India had been dishing out hundreds of crore as Haj subsidy as a gesture of goodwill towards minorities. Since the Haj Committee did not make any distinction between pilgrims who could afford it and who could not, who benefited from this gesture, whether the needy or the privileged, had always remained a debatable issue. Every year, after the operations were over, the MD would plead with the Ministry to stop the practice because the direct and indirect costs incurred by Air India including buying gifts to the pilgrims and detailing their technical and administrative personnel at various stations and setting up of new facilities at various stations far exceeded their recovery from the Haj Committee. Moreover, because of the damage caused to the interior of the aircraft, all the aircraft detailed for special operations had to be refurbished after the operations.

One Chief Vigilance Officer (CVO) posted to Air India (every PSU had a CVO appointed by the Chief Vigilance Commissioner) could manage, because of his nuisance value of which all MDs are afraid of, to visit all the stations all over the globe where Air-India offices are located with his wife and some of the attractive stations several times on free tickets. The primary task of the CVO is to prevent misuse of the resources of the airline and report on any misdeed of officers and staff of the PSU. Unfortunately, like many other CVOs, the CVO of Air India misused his powers to the maximum extent he could without any positive contribution to the airline. I was the only officer in the ministry who did not avail of free tickets from Air India for foreign jaunts with family during the entire tenure in the ministry.

Air India, being the national carrier, had always been responsible for the VVIP flights to foreign countries. During Nehru era, Pandit Nehru being a true democrat set a healthy tradition that only the First Class of Air India would be reserved for the VVIPs mainly the President and the Prime Minister of India whenever they visited foreign countries. I do not remember when this good tradition was broken, perhaps during the later part of Indira Gandhi's regime. A practice was established the entire aircraft would reserved for the dignitaries even if it meant putting out of operation 747-200 or 747-400, a 400 hundred seater aircraft. Subsequently, with increasing number of VVIP visits, sometimes for long duration, and increasing security concerns shown by the intelligence agencies, two Jumbo Jets were sanitized for VVIP flights and two sets of best pilots and crew members were taken off the normal duty roasters resulting in large-scale disruption, delays and cancellation of scheduled flights, which seriously damaged Air India's reputation and earned the name of unreliable airline. Every time the VVIP flights were scheduled, the aircraft was specially inspected and refurbished to make an office room with all gadgets and communication systems, a drawing room, bed rooms, and a conference room with teleconferencing facilities. The VVIP flight was always a big affair and also a source of patronage; a host of journalists, politicians and officials were invited to join the VVIP team in the flight. The entire group were expected to be "properly looked after" by Air India, in addition to the hospitality extended by the Indian Missions. Air India would entertain them with dinner parties, foreign liquor and gifts. While Air India did receive payments for hiring the aircraft by Government of India, and it was a pittance considering the future loss owing to disruption of services and loss.

When the bill for nationalization was brought in Parliament in 1953, JRD Tata met Pandit Nehru and pleaded not to nationalize Air India saying that with total government control, Air India would not be able to grow and would not be able to compete with the international commercial airlines. Tata's prophecy came true and by 1990s, Air India was reduced to an insignificant minor airline. With the abolition of the Air Corporation Act in 1993, the circle was complete.

III

Indian Airlines- Scandals Galore

One of the MDs of Indian Airlines, a close friend of mine confided that during his tenure, he will make sure that Indian Airline does not embark upon acquisition of new fleet of aircraft, even though modernization had become an urgent necessity because he did not want to face any CBI inquiry! His logic was simple; every time Indian Airlines acquired new aircraft, it was mired by kick-back scandal and every aircraft deal in the past had come under CBI scanner. The last acquisition of aircraft for IAC was made in 1980s and CBI was still questioning officials and continuing their investigation through the 90s. Therefore, nobody would stake his future career by venturing to modernize the fleet and would obviously wait for the successor to take such 'fatal' decisions.

One good thing about nationalization had been that Indian Airlines became one of the biggest domestic airlines of the world to have a vast network of air services bringing the remotest areas into the air- map where private airlines would never agree to fly, partly because of non-viability and partly because of technical deficiency. While the airline had a motley combination of old aircraft inherited from the private airlines, the latest being their own Boeing 737-200, Indian Airlines regularly operated flights from Srinagar to Car Nicobar and from Rajkot to Kohima. It connected remote areas of the North-East like Tezpur, Dimapur, Imphal and the Andamans. Thanks to the Second World War, at least 100 major and minor airports and a total of about 500 airstrips were built in all corners of the country.

In spite of having an old and ageing fleet, the safety record of the airline had been untarnished till 1980s. It had won accolades as one of the best and safest domestic airlines of the world. This was because the airline was fortunate to have a large number of highly skilled, may be world's best, pilots and engineers. Reputation of Indian Airlines received a set back with a couple of accidents –one involving Boeing -737 at Imphal while approaching the runway hitting a hill-top in thick fog and another involving Caravelle while landing at Delhi airport in bad light in the evening killing all passengers including a dynamic Minister of the central Cabinet, Mr. K.R. Kumaramangalam.

The major effort to modernize the fleet was taken in the 80s under Rajiv Gandhi Government. An expert committee headed by JRD Tata recommended Boeing-767 for Air India and latest version of Boeing – 737 for Indian Airlines because of compatibility, common repair and maintenance facilities and training of pilots and engineers. There was perhaps another important reason in the mind of JRD Tata whose integrity and intellectual honesty was unquestionable. Under the US

Anti- Corruption Law, any US Corporate resorting to any corrupt practice in their business deals were subjected to severe punishment including black listing by the US Administration. Therefore, there was practically no chance of receiving any kick- backs from the Boeing Company by any agency or persons or political group and the aircraft could be procured at a fair price.

The Tata Committee's recommendations were accepted but the decision was reversed at the Cabinet level. An unseen hand appeared to have worked in favour of Airbus Industrie. The government took a surprise decision of purchasing 30 Airbus-320 aircraft from *Airbus Industrie* in one go. This was more surprising considering the fact the aircraft did not complete the test runs with its new engine (V-2500) developed by them and other airlines were yet to place orders for this newest aircraft. India had the option of going for GE Engines which the US airlines did and perhaps, India would have done better had they opted for GE engines but they were lured to believe that the new engine was much more fuel efficient than GE engines, a claim which turned out to be untrue. The level of sophistication and automation was too much for the Indian pilots and too much reliance on 'fly by wire' led to the Bangalore crash in broad day light.

The decision to go for Airbus-320 against Boeings created a great storm of controversies. Rumours were afloat about a huge amount of kick back from the deal. Perhaps a non- controversial decision could have been to divide the orders and procure 50 percent of the requirement from Boeings and 50 per cent from Airbus. Later, under pressure, the entire deal was brought under CBI investigation. But, till now, the investigations could not point the needle of suspicion as to who received the kickbacks.

While Indian Airlines faced teething problems with the first batch of A-320 in the initial stages and later with the performance of V-2500 engines, in retrospect, it turned out to be a good decision. Sometimes, hasty and autocratic decisions are required to pull things out of the bureaucratic labyrinth of delayed decisions which come in trickles and not as a torrent to have significant impacts. It is believed that Rajiv Gandhi himself took the decision to induct 30 A-320 aircraft, the latest at that time, in one go so that Indian Airlines can easily move forward towards twenty-first century. This had been indeed a visionary decision because Indian Airlines suddenly got a new look and became one of the most modern domestic airline in the world. Indian Airlines did never in its history such a large number of modern aircraft in its fleet. Indian Airlines had been replacing their obsolete aircraft in ones and twos. It had inducted earlier a few of Fokker Friendship, a small aircraft and half a dozen Airbus-300, a 300 seater aircraft for connecting the Metro Cities of

Bombay, Calcutta, Delhi, Madras and also Bangalore and Hyderabad. Airbus-300 had been the workhorse for Indian Airlines for many years but its main problem was it was too big be operated in the majority of the airports and on the metro-routes, is was difficult to fill the seats. Therefore, there had been a long-felt need to induct a medium size fuel efficient aircraft of 150-200 seat capacity. Airbus -320 filled the gap and was ideally suited for operation to all the State capitals and also to the neighbouring countries and the Middle-East. For many years to come, Airbus-320 remained the backbone of Indian Airlines' fleet.

But the main problem confronting the airline had been not the availability of aircraft, not the lack of expertise, not the lack of training, not the lack of incentives but excessive obesity coupled with mismanagement and indiscipline. I used to ask what were the total sanctioned strength and the number of personnel actually in position. Nobody including the HRD people had any clue; the airline went on adding more and more people on ad hoc basis as and when required over a long period of time. One estimate was that about 5000 people are on the rolls of Indian Airlines. I was taken aback to discover in 1995 that at least 100 Consultants, mostly retired senior personnel, were working for Indian Airlines! The MD was so 'benevolent' that any retiring officer who approached him to be accommodated after superannuation could expect to get a consultancy job to prevent his sudden loss of income. Another surprising phenomenon I discovered was the existence of about 40 posts of Directors below the Board level making it almost a system of time-bound promotion for the senior officers. I could understand that the move was to placate the feelings of the headquarters officers who had a tremendous pay differential with the flying personnel some of whom (like senior pilots) would be getting more than Rs.36 lakh.

The excessive obesity coupled with the muscle power of the unions led to such a fat salary bill that Indian Airlines could not absorb leading to a debilitating diabetic situation for which no cure was in sight. Soon after I joined the Ministry, I was horrified to find that the wage bill exceeded Rs.900 crore, a 300 per cent hike from a level of Rs. 300 crore a year ago. Wages of all categories, especially the pilots, were increased 3 times after a series of wage negotiations. When asked about the reasons, the MD confided that during his tenure, he would not allow any industrial situation to arise as a result of failure of wage negotiations. His mind was very clear on this issue. All his predecessors who had faced industrial situations and tried to take strong actions against the unions had to face humiliation and ultimately had to make a dishonourable exit. Simply, there was no alternative but to adopt an appeasement policy because no government of the day, for political reasons, would wholeheartedly support the MD to take the unions head on.

Indian Airlines remained another story of governmental interference, indifference, inefficiency and gross nepotism.

IV

Sickness in the Sky

Liberalization initially created a near- chaos situation in the Indian skies. With the abolition of the Air Corporations Act and opening of the Indian skies to the private domestic operators, there was a stampede to get permission for import of various kinds of aircraft (mainly through lease or in collaboration with foreign airlines) to operate as separate registered private airlines. Suddenly, within a short time, the Indian sky was littered with a large variety of aircraft and a variety of colourful airlines. In the forefront were *ModiLuft* (in collaboration with *Lufthansa*), *Jet Airways* (registered in Isle of Man) and *Sahara Airlines* (Sahara Group). Subsequently, a number of airlines like *Kingfisher Airlines, Deccan Airways, Go-Air, Indigo, Spicejet, MD Air* etc. joined the fray. In addition, *Alliance Air*, a subsidiary of *Indian Airlines, Vayudoot*, a central Government undertaking to connect smaller cities and towns and *UP Air*, a State Government Undertaking started regular commercial operations.

What attracted the private players to enter the Civil Aviation sector was the glamour and eliticism associated with the industry. They thought owning an airline would confer them a high life, high profits and high prestige. Unfortunately, the majority of the entrepreneurs had no idea of the nature of the industry- the degree of capital-intensity, the complexity and sophistication of the operations, the extreme sensitivity and inelasticity of the business and the thin margin with which the industry operates. Those who had some experience did not have the capital and those who had the capital did not have the experience.

In the initial years, some of the airlines did extremely well. As for example, on the metro routes, *Damania Airlines* outsmarted all other airlines by their excellent service and on time performance. They even started serving liquor (which was confined only to international routes) to attract more passengers till it was stopped by the Director- General of Civil Aviation. They set a very high standard of customer satisfaction. After serving of liquor was banned on the domestic routes (which was always the norm in India), *Damania* started losing its clientele and with the enforcement of the Civil Aviation policy that all airlines were expected to operate at least 10% of their total flights in uneconomic and remote areas like the entire North-East India,

Jammu & Kashmir and the Andaman Islands, it had to discontinue services and became bankrupt.

One by one, almost all the major private airlines started losing money. Disillusionment with the glamour of the aviation sector came too soon and most of the airlines became sick. The first to go out of the market was Damania Airways. There began a procession of airlines exiting the sector. In the government sector, Vayudoot and UP Airways closed down their operations because of heavy losses and lack of expertise. Vayudoot was nicknamed 'Yamdoot' following a series of fatal accidents and extremely poor track record of air safety of its fleet mainly consisting of Dornier aircraft. There were incidents when the main door of Dornier fell off, sometimes, the door would not fully close and sometimes they would make emergency landing. Ultimately, passengers started avoided flying by Vayudoot, practically abandoning the airline leading to its closure.

This was followed soon by ModiLuft and East-West airlines and Sahara Airlines. ModiLuft started with big fanfare with a fairly good number of modern aircraft taken on lease from Lufthansa with whom they entered into a collaboration agreement. They established a market of their own with a good network of services, good customer care and good on time performance. They had to close down operations following a legal dispute with Lufthansa who seized their aircraft for non- payment of the lease charges. East- West Airlines, who also had created a good market in the metro cities and in the western and southern sectors, were embroiled in disputes with the law enforcing authorities who suspected their links with the under-world who funded them and who had links with the serial blasts in Mumbai.

The Ministry of Civil Aviation set up a committee headed by me to look into the reasons for the sudden sickness of the private airlines. The committee had interactions with all the airlines, heard their grievances and problems and came up with a voluminous report and gave a number of suggestions to correct the situation. The main reasons for sickness found by the Committee were - low capital base, inadequate working capital, lack of skilled personnel, lack of professionalism, greed and gross mismanagement. Of the factors which were beyond their control were high prices of Air Turbine Fuel (ATF) including high rates of sales tax, the compulsion to fly to difficult areas like the North-East and lack of common maintenance services and aviation engineers. The private airlines were all the time poaching on each other's pilots and engineers. The biggest poacher had been Jet Airways who had taken away a large number of pilots and engineers from Indian Airlines, who were lured by much higher compensations. A large number of technical and commercial personnel of Indian Airlines joined Jet Airways immediately on their retirement with a better pay package. The committee recommended that poaching on each other should be treated as unfair trade and be stopped. The committee gave a far reaching recommendation that the government should encourage only half a dozen established and well-managed airlines and not to allow 'fly by night' operators in the Indian sky. An analysis of the history of domestic airlines in major countries including USA strongly suggested that the competitiveness and complexities of the aviation sector did not allow more than half a dozen (actually 3 to 4) major airlines to survive and operate profitably in the domestic market.

Predictably, the Report known as Brahma Committee Report submitted to the Government was not acted upon and never saw the light of the day in spite of the appreciation and wide publicity received from the press.

There was another Committee headed by the then Civil Aviation Secretary, P.V. Jayakrishnan to look into the problems of air connectivity in the North East. The committee observed that forcing the airlines to fly a certain minimum percentage of their flying mileage in the North–East did not solve the problem of connectivity because all the private airlines were trying to complete the formality by touching Guwahati without going to the capitals of other states. The committee found that operations in the entire North–East region with a regime of low fares would never be viable and therefore, the states have to step in, first by reducing Sales Tax on ATF and thereafter, by subsidizing the actual loss incurred in inter-city services in this region as it is done for public transport services in the metro cities. The Jayakrishnan committee Report was again put into cold storage and needless to say, was never implemented.

The only major airline which escaped sickness was Jet Airways. Registered in Isle of Man, Jet had a meteoric rise and many questions were raised about its credentials, its sources of funds and the invisible hands behind the organization. No doubt, the airline enjoyed a great deal of political patronage. The Ministry itself had lots of doubts about it, but could not delve deeply into these issues because of its 'unseen influence'. It believed that a number of political heavyweights had invested their unaccounted money in the airline through Isle of Man but the truth was never known. From a mere 5 Boeing aircraft, the airline grew, within a period of 5 years into a giant airline having 30 jet aircraft and outshone all other airlines. Funds for the acquisition of new aircraft never seemed a problem for Jet; the only problem was the sanction of the Ministry for the new fleet. Their market share rose steadily and soon surpassed that of Indian Airlines thus becoming the number one domestic carrier. Subsequently, Jet received approval for flying out of India and got the distinction of becoming the first Indian private airline to become a domestic as well as an international airline.

I vividly remember one of the instances of the political influence it wielded because it involved me. Jet Airways wrote to the Ministry asking for a 'Comfort Letter' from the government to facilitate their External Commercial Borrowing (ECB) for the procurement of four more new aircraft costing millions of dollars. As JS&FA, I refused to issue such letter because it amounted to giving government guarantee for private borrowings which the existing rules did not permit. It had been the long-standing practice to grant government guarantee for foreign borrowings to government departmental and public sector undertakings making the government finally responsible for the repayment of debts in the event of default by the borrower. No such responsibility could be thrust on the state with the tax payer's money. The logic is very simple. PSUs are an arm of the government and their dealings including ECB were transparent and known while in the case of private operators there was no way of knowing if ill-gotten or black money was channelized through ECB or not. So I left office late evening giving the direction that the ministry cannot issue any comfort letter and that Jet could get, if they required, a letter from the DGCA, the regulatory authority about their credentials, fleet strength and viability which should serve the purpose.

Next morning, I was totally surprised to know that in spite of my observations and instead of approaching the DGCA, Jet did receive a Comfort Letter the previous night itself issued by some other Joint Secretary from some another desk which was irregular. The story told to me was like this. After I left office, some senior officer leaked my observations to the Chairman, Jet Airways, who immediately rushed to the Civil Aviation Minister and along with the Minister and the case file, went straight to the Finance Minister and within no time received the approval of the Finance Minister for the issue of the Comfort Letter which was done the same night. I never saw the case file during the rest of my tenure in the Civil Aviation ministry. After this incident, I shut my office doors for Jet officials including their Chairman. But, that hardly mattered with *Jet* who continued to receive patronage in spite of JS&FA.

But all said and done, I did have my silent support for the airline and had a deep appreciation for the professionalism with which it was being managed. Of all the airlines including Indian Airlines, Air India, *Kingfisher*, *ModiLuft* and *Sahara*, *Jet Airways* had been the only airline which was run and operated on professional lines. For this, the credit was due to their Chairman, Naresh Goyal who had been a wonderful administrator. This soft-spoken person was ruthless on inefficiency, slackness and indiscipline, be it on the part of the pilot, the cabin crew or the ground staff. Naresh Goyal had all the qualities of a good entrepreneur and understood the complexities and dynamics of the aviation industry, knew exactly what the passengers wanted, knew how to maintain his fleet in top condition, knew how to capture the market and also knew how to manage his finances to maintain profitability. Within no time, it won the hearts of the business community and the common public with its high standard of customer services and on time performance. Compared to them, Indian Airlines became a poor performer. Ironically, a large number of professionals were inducted from Indian Airlines, who could not really make a mark there. But, with his own discipline and innovation, he could convert the same people into good teams and efficient groups. Or compare them with *ModiLuft* which had a good chance of giving a tough competition to Jet but miserably failed mainly because one factor- lack of professionalism and lack of entrepreneurship; it was being run as a family-based ad-hoc non-professional organization. The MD of *ModiLuft* once confided in me saying that out of Rs.65 crore raised through public offering, he was asked to manage with Rs. 30 crore and the entire amount of Rs. 35 crore was kept out of business by the management all consisting of the members of the same family. Nobody knows where the money went! Obviously, they invited their own doomsday.

V

Liberalisation or New Windows of Corruption!

If people think liberalization or competition would eliminate corruption, they are mistaken, particularly in the Indian context. Indians possess infinite capacity to bypass and manipulate any system which comes in their way. It is always fashionable to blame the bureaucrats and the politicians for corruption in government; the common perception has been that government servants are more corrupt than others. But a deeper look will show a different picture. Once I mentioned to a retired Admiral whom I used to meet every day during morning walks at Nehru Park that I would like to join an NGO after my retirement for contributing something to the society, he was rather surprised and strongly advised in the negative. The Admiral added that he had worked for the government, for the private sector and also for the NGOs for considerable periods and his own experience had been that barring a few, the NGOs were highly corrupt; less corrupt was the private sector and the least corrupt had been the government sector because of the bureaucracy, a rigid system with rules and regulations, checks and balances and the system of accountability, CAG's audit and Parliamentary control. Government looks more corrupt because of its visibility and the media but corruption in the private sector or in the NGOs are never visible and known to the public.

But the fact remains that our bureaucrats including many top bureaucrats and many of our politicians have perfected the art of manipulating the system and misusing official powers for their own benefits. The question which will naturally arise is: who is to be blamed - the giver or the taker? Corrupt practices on the part of the bureaucracy and the politicians who are at the helm of affairs are crimes and cannot be condoned but what about those who initiate, offer by clever means and make use of all human weaknesses to achieve their ends? In order to get their things done, especially in winning contracts or speed up matters, the private sector is ever ready to bribe anybody, anytime, anywhere -often in cash but in many a case transfer of property, transfer of funds in foreign banks and exploiting individual weaknesses. The industrialists had come to the conclusion that bribery was the best and easiest way to get solutions. Some top industrialists told me about bureaucrats: 'everybody has a price and everybody has some weakness or other; we find out the weakness and exploit it'. I was surprised and challenged them 'ok, let's see if you can try to bribe me'! I became doubly cautious after this incident and almost became paranoid against our Indian entrepreneurs.

"One lakh per seat, what does it mean?" I quizzed my colleague. My colleague must have thought I was an idiot. Indeed, I was an idiot not to understand the mechanism adopted by the politico-bureaucrat nexus for looting the nation! One day I was told the minister had constituted an 'aircraft purchase committee' for the sole purpose of screening the proposals to increase in capacity or import of aircraft by the private airlines. That meant that no private airline, big or small, could place any order for purchase or taking on lease any new aircraft or change the structure of their fleet including increase in seats without the specific approval of the aircraft purchase committee and of the Civil Aviation Minister.

This was nothing but bringing back the infamous "License Raj" through the back door. While the stated State Policy was to abolish the "License Raj", nobody in the government did anything to interfere in the activities of the minister. I was most unhappy about this because I knew I was roped in to give legitimacy to many of the wrong-doings which were going to take place. When I resisted, I was told that as FA, I could not escape the responsibility; every such committee would have to necessarily include the FA. So, I had to attend all the meetings of the committee against my will. In many cases, my conscience would not permit to agree to the proceedings and I would offer my note of dissent. One day, my colleague who was made the convener of the committee came to my room and quietly told me -'why do you want to annoy the minister and incur his displeasure? You may not know that that minister has already decided about whom to give permission; the committee is expected to endorse his decisions. I am also helpless knowing full well that injustice was done in some cases and some parties were shown undue favour. By objecting to the proposals, you become a bad man.' I told him I was helpless because, as FA, it was my duty to see that rules were followed uniformly and the government looked fair.

I always felt that the business of giving permission for import of aircraft including importation on lease belonged to the Indian Customs Department who under the 'Rules of Business' of Government of India were the appropriate authority and the Ministry of Civil Aviation had usurped this power. But, I was told that the Customs Department, because of their lack of expertise in aviation business, had transferred the task to the Civil Aviation Ministry about which I was doubtful. One day, the convener confided in me and told me 'you don't know the real reason? It's because of one lakh per seat!' I was flabbergasted. I could not believe that the government system could be manipulated to such an extent to make personal gains. The buzz on the corridors of Civil Aviation was that unless one lakh per seat or Rs. 120 lakh for a Boeing-737-400 is paid to the political bosses, permission for the acquisition of the aircraft would not be granted to the private operators and only those operators who agreed to pay got the approval. This was not unthinkable to me nor did I get any proof.

I could only feel sorry for myself. An idiot like me had no place in such a system.

VI

Tata- Singapore Airlines Grounded.

Civil aviation was the only major industry which the Tatas carefully shunned ever since their flagship company Air India International was snatched away from them. Civil aviation occupied a special place and generated special sentiments in the hearts of the Tatas for a variety of reasons. Their supremo J.R.D. Tata was not only a pilot but an adventurer - he made the daring first solo commercial flight from Karachi to Bombay, which was unthinkable those days. He was the founder and pioneer of the modern aviation industry in India. He nurtured Air India International for a long time and made the airline the first all-jet airline in the world. He personally pleaded with Pandit Nehru not to nationalize the airline which he said would stifle the airline's steady growth. In spite of having an excellent relationship with Nehru and mutual admiration for each other, Tata's Air India International was nationalized to form Air India. In hindsight, it would appear that it had been a disastrous decision. Even today, Air India is gasping for breath.

In 1993, the Open Sky Policy was introduced and the Tatas could have easily re-entered the industry with a new airline and could perhaps have occupied the commanding heights in civil aviation again because of their corporate strength, commitment and vast experience in the field. Why did the Tatas not enter the industry again and scrupulously shied away from civil aviation remains a mystery. One can only conjecture that it was mainly because of their wounded feelings and also because of the disadvantages of a fresh entrant having to start the business from a scratch.

I always believed that after liberalization of the Indian skies, the Tatas had intense desire (though not expressed in public) to enter their favourite kingdom lost but for some reason or other, they were following a 'wait and see' policy. I was sure one day, they would come back with a bang and they were just waiting for an opportune moment to do this. The opportune moment did come soon when within a few years of liberalization, the private airlines, one by one, started getting sick and making unholy exit. Pressures mounted on the Tatas to start a domestic airline which would be viable, efficient and charge fair and affordable airfare.

The Tatas brought a big proposal to start a major airline in collaboration with Singapore Airlines, the airline which the Tatas helped develop by loaning a few aircraft and pilots from Air India International. The company was to be registered as an Indian company but Singapore Airlines would have considerable interest in it and would provide the state of the art technological support in its operation and maintenance.

Tata's proposal immediately alarmed the existing players in the sector. It was believed that by their very presence, efficiency, and reputation, Tata-Singapore Airlines would take away a substantial portion of the market share and would gradually edge out the major domestic airlines. It posed a 'real' danger to Jet Airways, Kingfisher Airlines and even the Indian Airlines. The best thing which should happen to the existing airlines was to 'kill' the proposal. All conceivable efforts and lobbying were made by the rivals to ensure that the Tata-Singapore Airlines does not get off the ground.

The Civil Aviation Secretary, Maharaj Kumar Kaw, an extremely upright officer welcomed the proposal and very much wanted that the Tatas should re-enter the industry. As Financial Advisor, I also tried to help the cause of the Tatas in a small way. A year rolled by but there was no indication of any progress as regards approval of the proposal. Meetings after meetings were held and the Tatas gave a number of presentations justifying their project and clearing the doubts. After a year, the Tata Officials in charge of the project got tired of visiting the Ministry and distinctively showed their frustration. In their meetings with me, I had informally suggested to them that as a strategy, they should scale down their proposal and start in a modest way with 4-5 aircraft the approval of which could be given by the Ministry itself and would not involve the long-drawn process of approvals by the Public Investment Board and the Union Cabinet. They did not listen to my advice and became more and more adamant and combatic - the whole of it or none. The end result was the Tatas did not get the nod from the government to start an airline. Here the government meant the Civil Aviation Minister.

The matter was not as simple as it looked. I suspected there were deeper reasons for not welcoming the Tatas in the Indian skies and the question of payment of a heavy bribe must have been involved. It was an open secret among the lobbyists and agents of the commercial airlines that introduction of a new fleet or expansion of an existing one was not possible unless a specified amount of bribe money was passed on at the ministerial level. Since the corporate policy of the Tatas did not allow them to pay bribe for promotion of their business, they had no alternative but to withdraw their proposal to start a new airline. Their withdrawal did not create a whimper, not even a ripple but a deep silence.

Many years later, Ratan Tata broke the silence in a press conference saying the actual reason for their unexplained withdrawal from civil aviation. He said he was asked to pay a bribe of Rs. 15 crore (150 million rupees, a big amount those days) to the politician in power to get the permission to start a new airline, a suggestion which he flatly refused. The government of the day lost no time to deny the accusation as white lie.

VII

Juhu Airport on Sale!

Whether it was sheer private business interest or a genuine concern for the Airports Authority's poor finances, there was a sudden rush of blood for commercialization of all airport lands. From a whispering suggestion, it gathered a momentum to become a loud slogan on the corridors of Rajiv Gandhi Bhawan, presumably emanating from the corner of the Minister's office. All welcomed it as new source of revenue which could help finance the pending proposals for airport expansion and modernization. But, surprisingly, the private sector was only interested in the properties located in Bombay and Delhi and among the two cities, Bombay.

The Airports Authority of India (AAI), following persistent pressures from the political bosses and their private discussions with the Chairman, started calling for open tenders for commercialization of airport lands. I was not aware if there was any other open tender floated except for the prime locations of Juhu airport. Two days before the scheduled meeting of the Board of Directors, the Executive Director (Finance) of AAI lands in my office with a bunch of papers for my perusal. I found him in a disturbed state of mind and knowing that he had been an extremely conscientious officer, asked him to unburden himself. I could guess that something very wrong was going to take place which his conscience did not permit. He showed me all the tender documents, the working and the evaluation papers and the Comparative Statement. On the face of it, everything appeared to be in accordance with the rules and in the normal course, the Board Members would not have reasons to cast doubts on the authenticity and fairness of the evaluation made. I also could not catch the snag. Then, he explained how the entire evaluation had been manipulated to favour a particular party who had close links with the minister.

A deeper look at the tender papers and the evaluation process revealed that the Airports Authority did not strictly follow the accepted procedure of two-bid system – the technical bid and the financial bid and resorted to financial bidding only. Out of about two dozen applications, ten parties were found eligible and were short-listed. By far, the best offer came from a reputed construction company based in South India. For mysterious reasons, this company sent a letter at the last moment withdrawing their offers from the bids.

Nobody knew the exact reason for this sudden and unusual move. It was speculated that some other party having lot of connections and muscle power either threatened them or persuaded them to withdraw their offer which would have made them the most eligible party. I agreed to review all the offers of the firms put on the short- list.

The firm which was put on top of the list by the evaluation committee apparently appeared to have offered the highest absolute amount but on application of the Net Present Value (NPV) formula to the revenue streams, they actually came third and the second and the third highest bidders needed to be placed above them in the short list. The evaluation committee very well knew about the actual rankings but manipulated the entire exercise so that the contract was awarded only to the firm which was close to the minister and whom the minister wanted the contract to be awarded. Obviously, the minister was promised huge personal gains from the contract by the prospecting party.

My analysis and my opinion on the deal and my comments in the form of a note of dissent on the Board agenda note, jointly drafted by the Director (Finance) and me, was a closely guarded secret till the Board meeting. In the Board meeting, the agenda item was placed towards the end (when the Members looked tired) giving the impression that it was a routine and innocuous matter on which detailed discussion was not necessary. At a point when a Board Resolution was about to be passed, I intervened giving a full picture about deficiencies in the evaluation process and the dangers of accepting such a proposal. Immediately, the Board woke up and decided to defer the agenda item and asked the Airports Authority to re-examine the proposal and re-evaluate the offers using modern scientific methodology. Needless to say, the proposal did not see the light of the day again.

The same evening, the minister who was anxiously waiting for the deal to come through, was suitably briefed by the Chairman about the Board's inability to pass the resolution and the persons responsible for this. He was visibly upset. He was so angry that he could not restrain himself from blurting out that "this FA should be taught a lesson". After this incident, this particular minister never spoke to me and openly tried to shift me out the Ministry through the Finance Minister (Dr. Manmohan Singh) who never agreed to shift his officer for doing his duty.

VIII

Government Subsidy for Haj Pilgrimage- to be or not to be discussed!

India is perhaps the only country in the world which provides cash subsidy for Haj pilgrimage to each person going through the Haj Committee. Nobody in the ministry could exactly tell the background and the circumstances under which the system of Haj subsidy with taxpayers' money was first introduced in "secular" India. According to Muslim scholars, acceptance of any form of cash subsidy for performing Haj pilgrimage is against the Shariat. This has also been the perception of the majority of the Muslims who believe that one should go for Haj on his own even if it meant selling his property. Ironically, the number of Haj Pilgrims accepting the subsidy and the quantum of subsidy went on increasing every year.

Under the Allocation of Business Rules, the subject of Haj Pilgrimage is allocated to the Ministry of External Affairs. But the subsidy amount was being budgeted for the last ten years in the Annual Budget of the Ministry of Civil Aviation. On my taking up this issue, Ministry of External Affairs would skirt the problem saying that it would be more convenient for the Ministry of Civil Aviation which controlled the airlines, to utilize the funds for air transportation of the pilgrims. Every year, the proposal for subsidy would be prepared and every year the Ministry of Finance would recommend to the Cabinet that the amount of subsidy should be progressively reduced with the object of eliminating the Subsidy within a few years. Every year, it would be pointed out that it was not appropriate for the Government to sanction cash subsidy which did not have religious sanction quoting the Shariat. But, every year, the Government, irrespective of political affiliations, would ignore the serious and rational objections and observations of the FA and the Finance Ministry and the Cabinet would sanction without discussion whatever money was asked for. No Government had the courage to stop or at least initiate a debate on the issue. It was obvious the vote-bank politics took precedence over every other consideration of governance.

In this connection, I am reminded of an interesting story. It had been the usual practice that every year, the Finance Minister addresses the Financial Advisors of all the ministries to take stock of the progress of spending and of the pace of implementation of the Plan projects in particular. In one of the meetings, the Finance Minister was very passionate about introducing Zero-Base Budgeting for all the ministries. He advised the Financial Advisors to take a hard look at all the Plan and Non-Plan Schemes and start immediately the exercise of reviewing the schemes *ab initio*. All non-essential and also non-performing schemes should be weeded out. The direction was very clear and the Financial Advisors nodded in appreciation as if a battle had been won. When the meeting was nearing conclusion (as usual, I always get a chance to ask the last question), I asked the Finance Minister if I could ask for a clarification from him. He agreed. I explained to him that in the Ministry of Civil Aviation, the bulk of the Budget (more than 150 crore) is spent on giving subsidy to Haj pilgrims. This is non-plan expenditure and whether I should review this scheme. He almost sprang on his chair and said 'no no, this cannot be discussed'. The entire hall became quiet. Many may be surprised to know that this Minister was from the BJP.

IX

Why is India a Poor Tourist Destination? It is the Toilets!

In spite of having a full-fledged Tourism Ministry, a Directorate of Tourism headed by a Director-General, a large number of Government Tourism Offices in foreign countries, a Tourism Development Corporation(ITDC), a chain of hotels and Hotel and Catering Institutes, India miserably failed to attract foreign tourists. On the dawn of the new millennium when a large delegation was sent to the last tip of the

Great Nicober Islands facing Indonesia to welcome the first ray of sunrise, arrival of foreign tourists remained more or less stagnant. While Sri Lanka, a tiny country could attract more than 5 million tourists every year, India could attract only around 2-3 million tourists which included NRI and expatriate Indians. This shows India in a very poor light as compared to what Spain or France had achieved. Spain and France attract tourists the number of which almost equals the size of their population i.e. 50- 60 million every year.

Either the officials of the Ministry of Tourism did not know the reasons or if they knew, they were not serious or were incapable of removing the bottlenecks. Ever since a separate Ministry of Tourism was created, this question was being debated in all fora of the government, the PSUs, the travel agents, national and international conferences but no concrete action plan had never been drawn expect some pious statements and targets made in the successive Five- Year Plans of the Ministry. Like many other Ministries of Government of India, this Ministry also existed for self-preservation rather than for aggressively promoting national interest in this area.

One of the Civil Aviation Secretaries, Mr. Yogesh Chandra with whom I had worked, an immensely practical person was never tired of his theory, a simple necessity that foreigners shy away from India simply because of the appalling conditions of the public toilets.

All foreign tourists, especially the female tourists find it extremely difficult to use the roadside toilets which are invariably found stinking, dirty, unhygienic and unfit for use. The foreign tourists hesitate to use toilets during road journeys and even in train journeys. Except for Rajasthan where 'mid-way' motels with decent toilet facilities have been constructed for almost every 100 kilometres on the national highways, in the nineties, tourists could hardly think of decent toilets on the national and state highways. The common perception was, as compared to the common facilities available in the USA where, apart from the integrated State Tourist Centres and the 'Exits' (which are mini-shopping centres) on the Inter-State roads, every gas station, every restaurant and every departmental store is required to maintain decent and clean toilets for common use by the visitors, the facilities available throughout the length and breadth of India had been rather primitive. This single bitter truth could not be accepted and faced by the people in power who could hardly understand the psychology and necessities of genuine foreign tourists.

X

A Foreign Tourist Office
for 18 Tourists!

One fine morning, the Ministry of Tourism received information that hundreds of packets containing tourist literature were lying for a long time in the cargo offices of Air India at Delhi and Mumbai airports. Soon it was revealed that the newly printed and revised tourist literature were to be sent to the various overseas tourist offices of Government of India, which did not receive the literature for two full years just because Air India did not care to lift them. No official of the ministry even cared to enquire if the literature reached the tourist offices or whether there was any query from the tourist offices as to why the literature did not receive them. Air India defended their inaction on the plea that necessary customs clearance had not been taken and that there had been no clear order or instructions for the despatch of specific consignments to the various foreign destinations. This incident amply showed the all-round callousness with which the Ministry officials and their subordinate offices were functioning.

The episode revealed another shocking phenomenon – the tourist offices hardly contributed to the cause of promotion of foreign tourism into India; the performance of some of the offices, especially in the American Continents, was abysmal. A full-fledged tourist office was operating in Buenos Aires but the number of foreign tourists from Argentina did not exceed 18 for several years in the 1990s.

A large number of tourist offices spread over five continents were found to be non-functional. But, they were maintained at a considerable cost draining away precious foreign exchange just because they became a great source of political patronage; officials in the good books of the ministers and senior officers were rewarded by the lucrative postings which carried considerable financial gains. So entrenched were the vested interests that even a talk of conducting a review of performance of these offices, not to speak of abolishing some of them, was not entertained.

I started a *suo motto* review of these offices and came to the conclusion that existence of at least six tourist offices could not be justified and therefore, needed to be closed. Within my mandate as Financial Advisor, I discussed the matter with the Expenditure Secretary followed by a letter pointing out the need to close down these offices and prevent the avoidable drainage of valuable foreign exchange of the country.

The reaction to my letter was anticipated. All efforts were made to hound me out of the ministry and also to spoil my confidential report. Fortunately, I was protected by the Finance Secretary. But, nothing was done by the ministry to prune the tourist offices which continued for eternity.

XI

Tourism Promotion - for India or Malaysia!

The Ministry of Tourism and its main arm the Directorate of Tourism were created with a view to serving as a catalyst in construction of new world class infrastructural facilities for foreign tourists and also in undertaking tourism related campaigns to attract tourists from all over the world. Towards this goal, the Ministry and the Directorate were supposed to work in conjunction with a common plan. As it happens with organizations, the principal objective remained unfulfilled and both the authorities took divergent means only to promote self-preservation. One instance will be sufficient to prove the point.

A proposal was floated that DG, Tourism needed to go urgently to attend a conference to be held at a sea resort of Malaysia and to deliver a speech on tourism. A speech proposed to be delivered by the DG had already been prepared by the Directorate. It had been the well-established practice in Government of India that all proposals of foreign visits by officials including those of Secretaries and official delegations would be scrutinized by the FA of the ministry before they were put up to Secretary and the Minister for their final approval. When the papers came to me for scrutiny, I was immensely amused about the whole affair.

The south-East Asian nations, mainly Singapore, Malaysia, Thailand and Indonesia had organized a conference to promote tourism in the region and main theme of the conference had been *how to attract Indian tourists to South-East Asian countries.* The obvious purpose was to woo away the vast number domestic tourists visiting places like Goa and Kerala to visit Singapore- Malaysia-Thailand circuit by offering much cheaper and more attractive packages. They invited India's DG, Tourism to give legitimacy to their 'poaching operations' and also to get sufficient insight as to how to do it. As subsequent developments had shown, these countries indulged in aggressive marketing alluring Indian tourists to visit exotic foreign destinations at the cost of Indian domestic tourism. This was certainly detrimental to India's national interest.

It was apparent that DG, Tourism did not read the theme paper and was happy to receive a warm invitation by organizers. He obtained verbal approval of the minister and also sent confirmation letter to the organizers about his participation. When all the facts and real intention behind the conference was brought to the notice of the Secretary, he was very unhappy, disapproved of the trip and informed the minister. The DG was obviously put in an embarrassing situation having confirmed his participation but he was left with no alternative but to cancel his trip on some assumed pretext.

Since that day, the DG stopped having any interaction with me and even stopped talking to me but never stopped in maligning me with his colleagues and my superiors. This was the prize which the FA got for doing his duty properly and conscientiously.

XII

Story of My Surprise Induction in Civil Aviation

I was all set to go for the supervision of audit of the United Nations University at Tokyo when orders came from the Government of India that I had been appointed as Joint Secretary and Financial Adviser in the Ministry of Civil Aviation and Tourism. For the last few weeks, I had been preparing myself well to go to Tokyo for the short assignment (which was for three weeks) collecting all relevant material, studying them and also making the travel arrangements. The Indian CAG had been elected for the first time to the UN Board of Auditors (the Board consists of three Auditor Generals of three continents) which undertake financial and management audits of all organizations and establishments under the control of the United Nations Organization located all over the globe. Among other audits allocated to the Indian CAG, the biennial audit of the UN University, Tokyo had been the responsibility of the Indian CAG who had the sole authority to choose the audit teams from his organization. The audit team for the audit of the UN University had been selected by him long back and I had been made the team leader. Just a few days before the team's departure for Tokyo, I was told not to proceed and a new team leader was appointed.

Surprised at the move, I went up to the CAG (C.G. Somiah) requesting that I may be allowed to complete the audit because I had made considerable preparations for this and that heavens would not fall if I joined the Ministry after three weeks. The assignment in Tokyo had been so attractive that I could have easily saved up to three lakh rupees in a legitimate way, which would have enabled me to wipe out my housing loans and fulfil my other financial commitments. But that was not to be; I had always been unlucky in monetary matters. Whenever I had tried my hands in the stock market or equity-based investments, I made heavy losses - in one or two cases, the companies became bankrupt. It appeared the CAG had already made up his mind. He reacted immediately saying that either I went to the Ministry as Joint Secretary or I go to Tokyo and asked me to choose one. I thought it was rather petty on the part of the CAG to have proposed like this because the two situations were not tradable. Obviously, he was under pressure to oblige some other officer. I was practically left with no option and decided to forego Tokyo in favour of Ministry of Civil Aviation.

I landed in Civil Aviation by accident and my selection surprised many, a cause of envy to a large number of competitors. Civil Aviation was considered to be a prize catch for civil servants who thought I must have manipulated well at the minister's level to get nominated for the post. The actual process of selection to the Central Secretariat had deteriorated so much that everybody started believing that unless you approach a politician, you are likely to be left out. The Civil Service Selection Board which selects officers for the secretariat posts had indeed been under constant pressure from the politicians. The unseen hand of a Minister, Chief Minister or a political heavyweight was always at work for the selection of every senior position and in some cases even for the selection of Deputy Secretary or Under secretary. One of my junior colleagues confided that he tried his best to oust me through the Chief Minister of Jammu and Kashmir but his intervention came rather late. I could discover that all the other Joint Secretaries in the Ministry working with me had indeed been selected with strong support and recommendations of the Chief Ministers of the respective states.

Therefore, my colleagues could not believe when I said that I had never approached any politician for my postings and transfers and that this also happened in the normal course. I could not blame them for their belief because the system had indeed degenerated to a large extent. I knew a powerful Chief Minister from a southern state, who would visit Delhi every month with a wish list which included names of his favourite officers of his own state to be accommodated in key positions at the centre. He would meet the Prime Minister and other concerned ministers with his wish list and surprisingly, in the majority of cases, he had been successful in his missions. Similarly, other influential Chief ministers and politicians mainly belonging to the ruling party would stand solidly behind officers of their states and do whatever they could to accommodate them, irrespective of relative merits, in the Central Secretariat. The task of the civil Service Selection Board had been made easier! The Board would always have a priority list of candidates with heavy tags who were necessarily to be selected for the key positions. Therefore, the Board was left with the task of selection to the minor and unpopular positions using their 'impartiality' and 'objectivity' of the selection process!

Many years later, I came to know that in my own case which I always thought happened in the normal course, there had been an element of grace from some quarters. The establishment officer in the Ministry of Finance called for names of only IAAS officers and other Accounts Service officers for the post of FAs who were supposed to have knowledge of financial rules and who were basically responsible to the Ministry of Finance. The intrusion of Administrative officers into this area had been minimal at that point of time. Subsequently, realizing the importance and central position of the Financial Advisor, all the posts of FAs in major ministries were upgraded and offered to the Administrative Service officers only, partly to accommodate many of them and partly, because of the powers they wielded. In my case, on receipt of the names from the Service Selection Board, this officer obtained the approval from the Finance Minister (Dr. Man Mohan Singh) before the panel was sent to the Civil Aviation Minister for his approval. Since my name appeared at the top of the panel and since the Finance Minister had already approved it, the Civil Aviation Minister was left with no option except to delay his approval or give a speaking order recording valid reasons for not accepting the nomination of the FM. In this case, the Minister did sit over the file for a few months providing room for manipulations which did not succeed. Till the Janata Government was in power, the process of selection and appointments was relatively free from political influences and had the stamp of sanctity and respectability thanks to the principled politics and toughness of Morarji Desai. After Rajiv Gandhi's death, there had been a steady erosion of political morality. Rapid politicization of the bureaucracy took place with the demise of true national leaders and with the advent of regional 'satraps', regional and caste politics engulfed the Central Government.

Chapter Three

Development Trough
Constructive Destruction!

I

India's Vanishing Forests

The British Administration left India relatively green. In 1947, more than 30% of the landmass of partitioned India was under forest cover and much of it was high-density forests. The British also left India with a healthy population of tigers, about 40,000, who are considered to be the biggest protectors of forests. That the Sunderbans remained relatively pristine and untouched for centuries was because the ferocious Royal Bengal Tigers did not allow human encroachments to take place in their territories and people were mortally afraid to enter the Sunderban area, the largest delta in the world, for poaching or any economic activity like agriculture, fishing or honey–gathering, not to speak of cutting down the trees.

The situation changed dramatically between Independence and 1990s. Within a period of four decades during which there had been wanton destruction of forests and the wild animals, before anybody could realize, India's forest cover came down to mere 13% and that too, with much thinner densities in most of the areas. The population of the protectors also came down to mere 2000.

The vanishing act started as early as 1947 when the country witnessed the largest human migrations in the history of the world. Millions of refugees started streaming into India from the west and the east. They had to be rehabilitated. The entire Terai region of the Himalayas (once famous for canes and bamboos), the pristine forests of Dandyakaranya (Orissa-Madhya Pradesh), the Andamans, Assam, Tripura and other areas of the North-East and North Bengal were cleared to create human settlements and agricultural land for the refugees.

India embarked on the Five- Year Plans from 1950 and during the First Five-Year Plan itself, a number of multi-purpose river-valley Projects with a chain of dams, reservoirs, and power houses and canals flattened large areas of forest land. Projects like Bhakra, Damodar Valley, Hirakud, Tungabhadra, Koyna, Periyar etc. engulfed thousands of hectares of forest land. As for example, the Periyar dam destroyed lush-green forests and converted the entire valley into a serpentine water body.

A major onslaught on forests started in 1956 when the Second Five-Year plan launched an ambitious plan for rapid industrialization and in the process to convert the predominantly agricultural society in to an industrialized society. Hundreds of public sector undertakings were established both by the Central and the State governments mostly on virgin or forest land. Mega projects like Bhilai, Durgapur, and Rourkella steel plants, Bharat Heavy Electricals Limited at Bhopal, Heavy Engineering Corporation at Ranchi with their sprawling townships and factories consumed large tracks of forest land. The process of industrialization continued through all the subsequent five year plans and accelerated considerably in the post-liberalization period. Large-scale mining activities, unregulated logging by forest contractors and economic exploitation of forest produce took a heavy toll on the forests.

But, the principal reason for the destruction of the forest areas had been the population explosion leading to human migration, expansion of agriculture, shortage of fuel wood, drastic decrease in wild life and disruption in the harmonious relationship between the tribals and the forests. The pressure on land and agricultural expansion pushed all forests and wildlife to small confines of the Reserve Forests and Wild Life Sanctuaries. During fifty years since independence, while the government was sleeping, the population of India increased almost three times (from 36 crore to almost 100 crore) and the forest cover shrank from almost one million square kilometres to almost 400,000 square kilometres.

The rural-urban conflict, the agriculture-forest conflict and the man-animal conflict went on increasing to a flash point when the government came up with a number of acts and rules to protect the forests, the wild animals and the bio-diversity of the country especially certain fragile areas like the Nilgiri Bio-sphere. One of well-conceived schemes to save the forests had been Joint Forest Management (JFM) under which all the people dependent on the forest for livelihood will have rights to harvest minor forest produce and a share of sale of certain produce like bamboo on the condition that they would protect the forest and do the necessary plantations for regeneration. While this had been a very good idea to involve people in forest protection, except in certain exceptional cases, JFM committees did not prove to be successful owing to obvious conflict and power struggle with the Panchayats and the greed of certain powerful people.

For example, the JFM could not prevent damage to the great Sunderbans. Ever increasing number of people tried to expand agriculture into the forest areas, to increase fishing activities and to harvest forest produce indiscriminately. The Bengal Government remained a mute spectator because they thought preventing people from having their livelihood from the area would be anti- people act. The result was the Sunderbans forest substantially shrank and the population of the Royal Bengal Tigers, thought to be invincible, also shrank slamming the state government's claim that the tiger population had increased.

II

India's Vanishing Tigers

All Indians hold their head in shame before the world community that independent India could not protect their own National Animal which once abounded in the length and breadth of the country. In fifty years since independence, the population of this majestic animal came down to mere 2000 from an estimate of 40,000 in 1947, almost at a point of extinction. India's new rulers, the intellectuals, the experts and the general public lost no opportunity in condemning the British rulers including the Viceroys and the Indian Princely States for promoting tiger hunting as a favourite sport which was responsible for killing of hundreds of tigers. Tiger hunting expedition had been on the menu of all of all visits of dignitaries, especially of the royalty from the British Empire. The criticism had been absolutely valid. But, those days, the awareness that tigers need protection did not exist because the number was so large that tiger population used to be treated at par with population of exotic birds. Even those days, there used to be murmurs of soft criticism against hunting but those were mainly on humanitarian grounds for senseless killing of these innocent majestic animals in an extremely deceitful and cruel manner. However, the net result of royal hunting on tiger conservation had not been too disastrous. In a span of 100 years, the British government could protect at least 50% of the tiger population in spite of sanction for hunting. During the first five decades of independent India, the government could not conserve even 5% of the of the tiger population left by the British in 1947. This is a sad and tragic story.

In post- independent India, the loss of tigers was directly linked with the loss of forests and the tiger habitats. With the gradual shrinking of the forest boundaries and scarcity of easy prey, the tigers were forced to stray into peripheral human habitation and started lifting cattle, which they found a much easier source of food than hard hunting within the forest. This created a serious man-animal conflict. They started resorting to an extreme step to poison the tigers. The poachers and the animal traders also took full advantage of the situation.

India's national governments, both Central and States, did not protect the king of the forest- the king was left to fight its own battle or bleed to death. In their lone battles, the tigers were fast losing their ground. News used to pour in about mysterious deaths of tigers in various parts of the country; a large number of deaths were not even reported. Animal activists like Maneka Gandhi and Valmiki Thapar were regularly giving statements and also brought it to the notice of the Ministry of Environment and Forests that every day, one tiger was being killed in India.

Neither the Central government nor the State governments gave credence to these reports and no effective steps were taken for tiger conservation. They dismissed the report of 'loss of a tiger a day' as exaggerated and fully relied on the reports sent by the State forest departments based on the faulty system of head count solely relying on the 'pug marks' of the animal. Valmiki Thapar proved to be correct when unofficial estimates by international bodies and the Government of India Census, 2001 were taken. Even 2001 Census exaggerated the tiger population and could not indicate the gravity of the situation. The tiger population in Sariska Tiger Reserve was being shown as 16 for a long time while the fact was that by 2001, the number came down to 6 and by 2005, all the tigers in Sariska were killed. I visited Sariska during an earlier period trying to spot a tiger with all the official machinery in place for full two days but failed to get any indication or clue that tiger survived in the forest. Subsequently, it was confirmed that that some notorious poachers had killed all the tigers of Sariska. Who should have been responsible for this? Is it the Forest Officer in charge or the State government or the Central government or the powerful poachers having links with international trafficking in animal products? There was no clear answer.

But, a part of the answer could be found in the scheme of things – the federal division of powers and the consequent division of responsibility. And, in an over-democratic set-up, divided responsibility is no responsibility. 'Forest' as a subject was kept in the State List leaving the entire matter of forest management and wild life to the lazy, indifferent and often corrupt State governments who had hardly any serious commitments to conserve nature, forest and wild life. The Constitution Makers could not perhaps envisage the importance of environment and forests in human survival and the human follies of wanton destruction of forests and wild life and if they had any idea about it, they would have certainly put the forests, the major rivers and the lakes under unified control of the Centre. The only saving grace in this area had been that the Central government could constitute an all-India Indian Forest Service (IFoS) for the administration of the Indian forests and forest resources, to which the State governments gave their consent. It is these officers who against all odds and threats to life from the poachers and mafia groups could salvage the situation in partly protecting the reserve forests and the protected animals.

But for the World Bank which gave liberal assistance for a unique project called 'Project Tiger' which was also supported and monitored by many international organizations like WWF (World Wildlife Fund), Tigers would have been long extinct in India. The 'Project Tiger' scheme which was carefully prepared in consultation with the international experts, created (curved out of the existing forest zones) a few special reserve forests exclusively for tiger conservations. The main tiger reserves so created were Sunderbans, Corbett Park, Ranthambore, Kanha and Bandhavgarh. There were many other forest areas like Simlipal in Orissa and Hazaribagh in Bihar where tigers could be found but they were not considered for inclusion under the Project Tiger Scheme.

The tiger reserves under project tiger were provided with special funding arrangement, advanced equipment, vehicles, monitoring systems and a dedicated group of forest officers and forest guards. A number of community programmes for the surrounding villagers and rehabilitation plans for the displaced tribals living within the forest areas were also included in the scheme. However, the implementation of the schemes was not without hurdles. The special treatment accorded to the tiger reserves including large flow of funds, privileges and incentives to the staff and providing special vehicles and equipment created lot of dissentions within the forest department and state government circles. Tightening of security in the parks made other groups of powerful people too unhappy- they were the poachers and the smugglers. All these groups of people and lobbies would vow to see that Project Tiger does not succeed on the ground.

At the central level, a new Division headed by a Joint Secretary level officer was created to administer the Project. A Project Tiger Monitoring Committee consisting of senior officials of the ministry, a few outside experts in the field and the World Bank Representative were also constituted to monitor the progress of the project. The Project Tiger Committee was supposed to meet periodically to review the progress of tiger conservation, discuss the serious issues, take decisions and send out instructions to the field formations for strict compliance. In 1990s, as FA of the ministry, I became a part of the Steering Committee and I found that the Committee was helpless in taking any important decision or to engage itself in getting its decisions implemented. In every meeting, people like Valmiki Thapar would bring all data and proof about how many tigers had been killed and how the Project Tigers had been negligent in tackling the onslaught of the poachers. In almost all cases, the forest guards were out-numbered or out-manoeuvred with their sophisticated weapons and tactics. The committee would patiently hear, make a note of the happenings, show sympathy and do nothing. It was the same story in every meeting. The committee was nothing but a lame-duck body and the ministry itself was nothing but a paper tiger.

The Project Tiger had been immensely successful in the initial years till the eighties when the tiger population surged. This was not because of the ministry, the state governments or of the project directors. This was because of one person and that person was none other than Indira Gandhi who had great concern for the environment especially the tigers. Indira Gandhi was the first Prime Minister and major world leader who attended the first Copenhagen Summit on Climate Change when the other world leaders were blissfully unaware of the great dangers of Climate Change and Global Warming. The keen personal interest which Mrs. Gandhi took in tiger conservation was amazing. She would periodically meet the Project Directors at her residence and would personally monitor the progress and developments taking place in the Tiger Reserves. Once, during my visit to Sariska Tiger Reserve, I was having a chat with Fateh Singh Rathore when he told how Mrs. Gandhi used to handle all problems of Project Tiger. She would call the individual project directors to Delhi, discuss the problems one-to one and issue instructions bypassing the Central Ministry of Environment and the State Governments. That is how Fateh Singh could do wonderful work for the Ranthambore Tiger Reserve.

After Indira Gandhi's death, no Prime Minister of India took personal interest in tiger conservation. The usual bureaucratic lethargy, lack of vision and criminal inaction returned too soon in this sphere also. Even those project directors who had direct access to the deceased Prime Minister were victimized. I was shocked to know even Fateh Singh Rathore who made a mark for himself and also wrote valuable book on the Indian tigers had been placed under suspension for certain minor indiscretions.

With lack of patronage at the highest level and dwindling of foreign funds, the tiger reserves were left at the mercies of the corrupt and incompetent state administrations and the situation reverted back to the pre-Project Tiger days. Instead of improving the conservation, the situation worsened and the tiger population started dwindling faster after 1980s. Caught between the dual control of the Centre and State and due to State governments' lack of commitment on providing the best of well-equipped personnel to protect the Parks from the onslaught of the mafias, the poachers and the delinquent villagers, the tiger reserves suffered irreparably.

I always thought, unless we follow the US system of scientific conservation and the system of security with an independent dedicated force, we cannot really protect our tiger reserves. We are too dependent on the callousness and incompetence of the State governments who do not mind living on falsehood. As for example, the West Bengal Government had been giving a picture for decades that the Royal Bengal Tigers were absolutely safe in the Sundarbans and their numbers were rising every year till their claims were proved totally wrong in 2011 Census which showed maximum rate of decline of tigers in the Sunderbans. In fact, the West Bengal Government had been sending to the world unscientific and unverified data on tiger conservation in the Sunderbans.

The existing system of conservation and dual control has been responsible for the total extinction of tigers from Sariska and Panna Reserves and partial extinction from many other Reserves like Kanha and Rajaji Parks. If the present system of administering the Parks continues, a day may arrive when, like the Cheetahs, our national animal will vanish from the Indian sub-*continent.*

Man is the greatest destroyer of nature, but it is the man who has the intelligence to save nature from disaster. Will man use his intelligence to save the tiger and prevent the disaster of extinction of the most majestic species called *tiger?*

III

What Made *Sunderban* Tigers Man-Eaters?

Normally, in the jungles, the tiger is not a man-eater and does not attack human beings unless provoked. Man may be mortally afraid of tigers but tigers are not afraid of man; perhaps they pity man. Tigers become man-eaters only under compulsion in certain circumstances: (a) when there is acute shortage of prey in the jungles; (b) when their habitat is destroyed by natural disasters or encroached upon my man; (c) when a tiger is seriously hurt and cannot hunt; and (d) when they become old with tooth decay and cannot eat bigger animals.

The only known exception to this rule has been the Sundarban tiger. It is believed that almost all the Royal Bengal Tigers of the Sundarbans spanning over the vast areas of the Bengal Delta on both sides of the borders of India and Bangladesh are man-eaters. The real reason is not known and still remains a mystery. There are a bunch of theories but it has not been possible, because of practical reasons, to test them on these tigers or in the laboratory.

Stories are galore of tiger heroics in the Sundarban area not heard in any other tiger lands. There have been cases where the tiger gives a huge jump into the river and takes away fishermen from the moving boats. Again, there are cases where the tiger, in the dead night, swims to the other side of the creek and quietly 'kidnaps' passengers sleeping on the roof of the launches without any body's notice. There have been cases where the tiger tiptoes from behind and silently takes away one of the members of the honey gatherers or wood cutters without the immediate knowledge of the others. Cases of cattle lifting or lifting of people sleeping outside on summer days in the peripheral villages have been too common.

Wildlife experts in India believe there are two possible reasons for this peculiar phenomenon. The first reason is: this is the only place in the world where the tigers have been pushed too close to the seas, on a vast marshy and salty wetland crisscrossed by rivers and backwater inlets. There is no grassland or bush-land where the tigers can easily hunt. Sources of freshwater like freshwater streams and freshwater lakes are practically non-existent in the south deltaic forest region. All the waters in the rivers and the backwater inlets have become more and more brackish over time with greater incursion of the salt waters from the sea. The tigers have no other alternative but to perforce drink the brackish water all the time whether they like it or not. It is believed which may be correct from the scientific point of view that excessive intake of salt have left the Sunderban tigers with elevated blood pressures.

The high blood pressure coupled with inhospitable habitat, heat and humidity and lack of happy hunting grounds made them irritable and extremely angry animals.

The second possible reason is the very existence of the mangroves over vast areas of Sunderbans, which the tigers hate to live with but cannot avoid them because of compulsions of survival. There is no other place on earth, where tigers are locked in a mangrove jungle. In fact, tigers should not have been in the Sunderbans and it still remains a mystery as to how tigers (later named by the British as Royal Bengal Tiger) believed to be the most gracious in the world landed in the Sundarban jungle which was one time cut off and isolated from the rest of Bengal. Some experts think that the Sundarban tigers must have come from the same stock of Siberian tigers, the biggest in the world in size, because of their striking similarities. Others think they are the cousins of the Kumaon tigers.

How could Siberian tigers reach the Sunderbans? It may sound like a fiction but not improbable. There was a time when the entire Asiatic region was home for millions of lions and tigers. It is possible that owing to their increasing numbers, groups of Siberian species, travelled through the forest corridors of Mongolia, China, North East India and Bengal and landed in the deep forests of the Sundarbans from where they could not get out.

The other theory is that a few tigers or even a couple were accidentally washed away by the flood waters of the Ganga (when some tributaries of the Ganga used to pass through this region) and got stuck in the creeks of the Sunderbans. The swampy rain forest could not be natural habitat for the tigers but finding no escape routes, they adjusted to the climate and the terrain and started breeding fast to become perhaps the largest family of tigers in one place (both parts of the Sunderbans in India and Bangladesh).

Whatever has been the credibility of these theories, the fact remains that tigers would have never made the Sunderbans their habitat by choice. It must have happened by an accident. The tigers could quickly acclimatize themselves and adjust to the hostile situation. They became master swimmers even in the strong currents of the rivers. Since they did not have open spaces and grassland for hunting which was limited to wild boars and stray groups of deer in the absence other bigger animals, they started to depend increasingly on the river resources mainly fish and sometimes crocodile or shark. They would perforce drink the brackish water of the rivers. When they could not get enough fish which would dwindle because of large-scale fishing by the fishing boats, they would, in anger, not hesitate to hunt their rivals, the fishermen.

One thing the tigers of Sunderbans could not negotiate with was the mangrove. Mangrove trees, unlike other trees, have adopted a unique system of propagation, not through seeds, not through shoots but through the roots which they flung skyward like spikes in the surrounding areas. The mangrove spikes badly hurt the tigers on their paws, legs and the body making them highly irritable and less agile for hunting. Their natural food there i.e. fish is depleted by the fishing boats and not enough source of food, they opt for easier prey, the fishermen. Since the bulk of fish is taken away by the fishermen making their life more and more difficult, they take revenge by attacking human beings which they would not have done in the normal course. It is believed that the mangroves which constantly hurt and irritate the tigers and the intake of salt water which cause high blood pressure perhaps contributed to Sundarban tigers turning into man-eaters.

IV

Draconian Act but Toothless

The Environment Protection Act was passed in 1986 with great hopes of restoring the glories of our national rivers, the lakes, the mountains, and the sea shores. It was a comprehensive Act aimed at prevention of pollution of air, water and soil of the country with special emphasis on pollution in the urban areas; it also contained directions for better management of hazardous material, solid waste management and effluent plants. It contained extremely strict provisions for punishment, termed draconian by many legal experts, for violation of the Act.

The chief architect of the Act was T. N. Seshan, the former Chief Election Commissioner, who was the Environment Secretary at that time. Seshan belonged to that breed of bureaucrats who did not believe in hearing others' voices and expected everybody to hear his voice, basically having a dictatorial mind-set. Such a mind-set, even in a democracy, is not always bad and in fact, sometimes necessary to push things for public good when there are too many opinions and a consensus is fractured. But the difficulty with such a mind-set is that it is likely to be misused. Quite contrary to the big public image they create for themselves as iron rulers, many of them suffer from delusions of super-ego and internal contradictions and would not mind prostrating before the political bosses for their own advancement but would be unforgiving to their juniors.

A living example of this was available in the Environment Ministry. Samar Singh, an IAS officer of Madhya Pradesh cadre, considered by his colleagues as an ideal civil servant with a high degree of integrity, efficiency and public concern had been the Additional Secretary of the ministry but was victimized because of his independent opinions. His confidential reports were spoiled and he was not considered for appointment as Secretary to Government of India. Samar Singh fought a lone battle in the court of law and the court restored his seniority and honour. But such was the moral strength and self-respect of the officer that he refused the offer of the Government of India to make him a Secretary; he fought the battle against injustice and having won it, he showed his magnanimity. His exemplary courage goes to show that everything is not over with the Indian bureaucracy. There is a silver-lining in the dark clouds of Indian bureaucracy and there were still officers like him, M. G. Pimputkar and Abhas Chatterjee, though very few.

There was no doubt that the Environment Act of 1986 was draconian; it was deliberately made so considering the enormity of the problem of all-round environmental destruction and degradation undermining the quality of life of all citizens of the country. But nobody gave serious thought as to how it should be implemented and what should be the institutional mechanism for effective enforcement of the draconian provisions of the Act. A number of organizational structures were created with a view to implementing, rather administering the Act in the usual manner as the bureaucracy proliferates. Each state created a Department of Environment and Forest in the Secretariat and a State Pollution Control Board. At the Central level, a Central Pollution Control Board with a battery of experts, supervisors and technicians and testing laboratories was constituted to study and monitor environmental pollution for the whole country and also initiate action against the offenders strictly following 'the polluter pays' principle.

But, none of the high-powered Pollution Control Boards was equipped with enforcement powers; they were practically powerless and toothless. They had to depend on the same general police forces of the states, for which environmental crimes would receive the last priority. To expect effective and prompt punitive action from a police force largely perceived by the public as ill-trained, ill-equipped, non-professional, corrupt and criminalized would be asking for the moon. The Pollution Control Boards should have been entrusted with the powers of enforcement. In the present situation, none of the offenders has been prosecuted for murdering the Ganga by the tanneries of Kanpur and for destroying the Yamuna by the industries of Delhi. It speaks volumes for the non-enforcement the 'draconian Act' when we find that not a single offending industrialist has so far been sent to the jail for deliberately flouting the provisions of the Environment Act, 1986.

V

Animal Trade, Poachers and the Government

Animal trade is a dangerous game which hardly receives serious attention from the public and the governments. This is as dangerous as international drug trafficking about which the whole world is aware but very few are aware of this illicit trade and fewer are involved in stopping it. The smugglers are smarter than the law enforcement agencies. The trade is ruled by powerful mafias organized on the pattern of the drug mafias with an international network across the globe.

Any sane person in the world would ask the question – why should wild animals be mercilessly killed for animal trade and why should it not be stopped? There is no easy answer. This has been a lucrative trade and no trade can perhaps be totally stopped by any government, however powerful they are, if there are demands for the products. The demand for animal products owes its origin to the concepts of social status and fashion but mainly to the supposed mythical medicinal properties and social practices. A large number of Chinese people believe that Chinese traditional medicines containing parts of rhino horn would give supernatural sexual powers or at least enhance their sexual abilities. This belief is propagated by the practitioners of traditional Chinese medicine. Similarly, in India, there are widespread beliefs that consumption of various body parts of tigers including tiger meat would cure many diseases and bestow additional strength and power. There is also a belief that sitting on a tiger skin and doing yoga or meditation on it, as the Indian Sadhus do, would give additional benefits. All these die-hard social beliefs in various countries have created sufficient demands for the wild animal trade.

Scientific experiments and investigations have proved that these beliefs are nothing but myths and there is no evidence to show that rhino horn enhances sexual power or the tiger meat can make a boy stronger or cure any disease. One of my office peons, a UP Brahmin and a strict vegetarian, who lived in the outhouse of my bungalow at Allahabad, had three sons and the eldest was very weak and sickly. One day, he came up to us to say that he would not be available for a week as he was leaving along with wife and children for Lucknow and his village home for the treatment of his eldest son. On his return to Allahabad we asked him about the kind of treatment his son received there. With a great deal of hesitation, he said that the village doctor had given a few pieces of tiger meat to be taken over a period of two weeks and thereafter, it was to be repeated a few times. Obviously, the treatment was quite expensive and everybody in the business was earning windfall profits. Needless to say, the treatment with tiger meat did not make any difference to the boy who continued to remain as sickly and weak as before.

Mythical beliefs, traditional medicine practices, status symbols and fashions of rich people have kept the clandestine trade in wild animals and birds still thriving. The most vulnerable animals who are the worst victims of poachers are the tigers, the elephants, the leopards, the rhinoceros, the musk deer, the Himalayan goats and the rare snakes. Every year, hundreds of these innocent and majestic animals are mercilessly and needlessly killed for profit without any consideration that one day, these animals may be totally extinct from the face of the earth. The poachers with their sophisticated weapons, better tactics and intelligence were always ahead of the state forest guards who were often unarmed. I did not come across of any case of any poacher being shot down by the forest guards in the act of poaching while there were many cases of forest guards being shot down by the poachers.

The question is – what was the government doing? The plain answer is: nothing much. The Ministry of Environment has a full-fledged Wild Life Division headed by a Forest Service Officer of the rank of Additional Secretary. Based on the recommendations of many high-powered committees, the division had drawn up a comprehensive plan for the conservation of the wild life in the Indian forests. They were clamouring for passing a Law which would have a three-pronged long-term strategy- (a) making poaching and trading in wild animals a serious offence deserving harsh punishment, (b) raising a force of armed guards to protect the wild life sanctuaries and (c) empowering the officers for seizure and prosecution on the lines of the Customs Officers.

The report was allowed to die its own death, so were the wild animals. No action was taken by the Central Government for a decade. In the mean time, reports were pouring in about daily killing of tigers and other animals and about the helplessness of the forest guards. The state governments almost abdicated their responsibility in Kaziranga, Hazaribagh, Sariska and even the Sunderbans. The ineffectiveness and lack of will power on the part of the state governments led to a sharp decline in wild life population, especially the tigers, which came down to an extremely dangerous level.

The reason shown by the Ministry of Environment as well as the Ministry of Finance for not creating an empowered and a dedicated force had been the usual argument that the government did not have funds to create and maintain such an armed force. This argument given in a routine and casual manner was not borne out by facts. The fact of the matter was that the Ministry of Environment & Forests had been surrendering more than 100 crore every year after for not being able to spend the allocated funds for their plan schemes and programmes.

It is the lack of understanding of the real problem by the ministers and the bureaucrats, insensitivity and lack of commitment of the officialdom, lack of patriotism and lack of initiatives to improve matters that came in the way of an effective enforcement system and left the wild animals in the national parks and reserves at the mercy of the poachers and criminals. In the absence of any effective deterrence, the killing spree continued.

VI

The Holy Ganga –
Not a Drop to Drink!

Since time immemorial, the Indians have treated and the majority are still treating river Ganga as the holiest of all rivers. There is a strong belief the Ganga water never pollutes and purifies itself. People have seen that Ganga water kept in bottles and jars for years remain crystal clear, does not collect sediment and bacteria cannot grow in it. This gave the belief that there is divine power in the Ganga water without which no religious function of the Hindus at homes, communities and temples is complete. At the end of each function, it is obligatory to sprinkle Ganga water called *Shanti Jal* on the heads of all people present with chanting of "Om Shanti" mantra which says "let there be peace to all people, peace to the forests and the natural world, peace to the earth and peace to the outer worlds in the universe".

This age-old belief gets a rude shock when people visit the Ganga at Kanpur, Allahabad, Triveni Sangam, Varanasi, and further downstream at Patna and Kolkata where Ganga water is not fit even for bathing. At Allahabad, we had a neighbour, a 70 –year old Bengali lady who wanted to have a good dip at Triveni Sangam was totally disappointed for not being able to do so because the Ganga was in full spate and had to be satisfied with drinking Ganga water to her heart's content. She had an unshakable faith that Ganga water cannot be impure and would certainly act like an elixir. Next day, she was bed-ridden with serious diarrhoea and with great difficulty, the doctors could revive her.

The Ministry of Environment created a large division for the 'Ganga Action Plan' headed by an Additional Secretary with a huge budget. It was a multi-prong project with a string of programmes and schemes aiming at bringing back the pristine glory of the Ganga and save the Ganga for the future. The programmes were in operation since the 1980s and hundreds of crores had already been spent on various schemes spread over the entire Ganga basin starting from Gangotri to Sagardwip. Funds were sanctioned by the Central Government but the specific schemes had to be implemented mainly by the state governments of Uttar Pradesh, Bihar and West Bengal.

Before the new millennium began, the Ganga Action Plan had already completed 15 years and therefore, many people started questioning about the wisdom of the project and whether there had been any visible improvement in the conservation of the sacred river and its water quality. The Central Pollution Control Board (CPCB) was entrusted with the task of monitoring the water quality of the Ganga. They also had set up a few monitoring stations at certain strategic places. They sent periodical reports which indicated that the water quality of the Ganga had generally been improving but the progress was very slow. Sometimes, they would be thrilled to report that many dolphins and turtles released in the river had been sighted near Varanasi or Allahabad drawing the conclusion that water quality and the oxygen demand must have improved.

But the ground reality told a different story. The CPCB had been sending only those doctored reports which would have pleased the bosses at Delhi and which the ministry would like to hear. The public perception had been the opposite. The public, the environmental activists and the voluntary organizations, felt that far from being restored, the condition of the Ganga was fast deteriorating. The whispers must have reached the ministry and therefore, not fully believing in the official story, the Environment Secretary, Mr. T.K.A.Nair who remained the Principal Secretary to the Prime Minister for a long time, decided to make a sojourn to the Ganga Valley on his own. On his return to Delhi, he immediately called a meeting of all senior officers of the Ministry of Environment and Forests. He looked visibly distressed and gave a vivid account of his visit urging everybody to do his bid to correct the situation. His descriptions of the reality at the ground level went like this.

At Kanpur, the tanneries were, against the existing orders, merrily dumping the untreated toxic waste into the Ganga and there was nobody there to tell them not to do so, least of all, to prosecute them. Common Effluent Treatment Plants (CETP) had been constructed but none of the CETPs were in working condition, partly due to technological problems and partly due to lack of electricity. Since these plants required substantial investment and their maintenance was also an expensive proposition, it was thought that sharing of costs among the tanneries would make lot of sense and there was no reason why the system should not work. Unfortunately, common responsibility was nobody's responsibility and the system became non-functional because of disputes, non-payment by smaller ones and lack of common administration. The end result was hundreds of tanneries at Kanpur were daily throwing tons of foul and toxic waste water making the Ganga at Kanpur most polluted, unfit for swimming and bath not to speak of drinking, and even making it unfit for the common river fish to live.

Mr. Nair's voice got choked when he started mentioning about the horrifying sight to which he was a witness, of dead bodies - some half-burnt and some un-burnt - floating all along the Ganga. The reasons were not far to seek. The poorest section of the people living on the banks, who cannot afford the cost of cremation throw away the dead bodies of their relatives into the Ganga believing that immersion in the holy river will earn the same kind of blessings as cremation for the after-life of the deceased. Another reason was non-availability of crematoria, especially electric crematoria, in many places.

As part of the Ganga Action Plan, a large number of electric crematoria were to be constructed in all municipal towns and cities from Haridwar to Diamond Harbour. Mr. Nair discovered during his visit that none of the crematoria at Kanpur and Allahabad was functioning. Asked why they were not working, promptly came the reply that the Electricity Board had stopped supplying electricity because of non-payment of bills. The reason for non-payment of bills was that the Municipality did not have funds which were to come from the government and the state government was not bothered to release the necessary funds on time. At his personal intervention with the concerned authorities in the state government and the municipality, Mr. Nair could get one or two electric crematoria re-stared but, this was no permanent solution to the problem which was likely to surface again and again unless a good system of operation and funding was devised. Another inherent problem associated with electric crematoria had been the low acceptance of the practice of burning bodies with electric power rather than by wood. Social acceptance of the new practice not sanctioned by the traditional religious beliefs has been very slow and also limited to major cities. Even in bigger cities like Varanasi or Allahabad, there would hardly be any taker for the electric crematoria. Therefore, even when these crematoria are fully functional, they will remain largely unutilized except in more liberal regions like Kolkata where the majority of the people prefer cremation in the electric crematoria rather by a clumsy and time-consuming burning process which creates an unbearable sight.

It was clear that sighting a few dolphins and turtles did not purify the Ganga water. With increasing siltation, weakening flows, pollution and rising of the river bed, the Ganga was in a real danger of shrinking and was unable to purify itself. The tall claims made by the Ganga Action Plan Directorate were not borne out by facts. In fact, there had been demands in some quarters that the entire Ganga Action Plan scheme should be scrapped and replaced by a better scheme. Hundreds of crores of rupees spent on the scheme have really gone down the drain!

VII

The Mythical Yamuna – the Dead River

The Yamuna is a river of eternal love. So much of history, philosophy, folklore, mythology, art, culture and specially, the inseparable images of '*Radha- Krishna Leela*' and of the Tajmahal are associated with the Yamuna that people refuse to accept the death of the river. They would still like to believe that the same romantic Yamuna still flows as it flowed when Lord Krishna used to play the flute sitting on its bank.

Look at Yamuna from any of the bridges at Delhi, your heart will cry out; you will be greeted with a stinking smell worse than any of the flowing drains. The entire stretch from Delhi to Agra and far beyond, Yamuna has turned into a stinking drain. I could not find any fish or turtle swimming in the Yamuna from Delhi to Agra and a river where fish and turtles cannot survive is a veritable dead river. I used to wonder how the policy makers, rulers and millions of people living on both sides of the Yamuna had accepted the situation in utter silence. In any other advanced country, in a similar position, I think there would have been an open revolt by the people who would have forced the government to reverse the situation. But, in a democratic India, everything is tolerated because the people have infinite patience, are resigned to their fate and survive with the cynicism '*sab kuch chalta hai*'.

Plans after plans had been drawn up by the Ministry of Environment with the active assistance of the World Bank to clean up the Yamuna mainly through construction of CETPs which would prevent untreated industrial sludge and municipal sewage flowing into the river and also through construction of oxidation ponds at various places. But nothing improved during the last three decades; on the other hand, the condition of the river went from bad to worse. The overflowing population of Delhi which increased from 4 million to 17 million in five decades, spilled on to the river fronts, the migrant population occupying large parts of the riverbed for habitation. Finding that Yamuna has been emasculated to such an extent that it was incapable of causing floods, the immigrant workers merrily established settlement colonies along the river.

The CETPs never really worked. The oxidation ponds slowly died out and gave way for housing colonies. The untreated industrial waste water and the sewers of entire Delhi and of the surrounding towns continued to flow into the river. On the other hand, in order to meet the ever-increasing demands for water from an ever-increasing population, more and more water was being drawn out of Yamuna. The barrage constructed north of Delhi diverted almost the entire water of Yamuna to meet the drinking water needs of Delhi and choked the river to death because there was hardly any water left for the free flow the river. The flow which still continued was nothing but a mixture of sewer water, industrial effluents and sludge, waste materials of the cremation grounds, garbage and plastics. Occasional mass campaigns to clean up the river have had only ritual values.

I have never seen in the world a river dirtier than Yamuna. It is virtually a flowing drain occasionally getting a life-support from the upstream dams and barrages which are forced to release surplus water in the monsoons causing overflow of its banks and irrational floods. But for all practical purposes, the Yamuna is dead. It is doubtful if the Central government and the Delhi government will ever be able to revive and restore the Yamuna to its glory as has been done for the Thames in London and the Seine in Paris.

VIII

Carrying Capacity of Delhi

Wastage of public funds- is anybody concerned with? Reports of experts- is anybody interested in taking action on? The people may be interested. But, this cannot be expected of the governments which are too busy in self-preservation and self- enrichment in a whirlpool of election politics.

With noble intentions, in 1990s, the Government of India had asked the National Environmental Engineering Institute (NEERI), Nagpur to undertake an arduous study on the Carrying Capacity of Delhi, which sought to understand what would be the optimum size of population Delhi could sustain in the long run depending on its basic resources – water, electricity, transport, infrastructure, housing, educational and medical facilities etc. The idea was to build Delhi a world class model city and for that it was essential to know its strengths and weaknesses. The report was to serve as the important input for the formulation of Delhi's Master Plan.

NEERI took several years to study all the aspects and factors concerning Delhi's future development. The voluminous report projecting a futuristic view was submitted to Ministry of Environment and Forests was submitted in mid-1990s when I chanced to see the report. The report contained a wealth of information collected and collated painstakingly over years' of technical evaluation. It contained a large number of practical suggestions for the policy makers.

The NEERI Report cost the exchequer 6 crore. After the report was submitted, the usual process of analyzing the report, examining the recommendations and initiating of action was completely forgotten. Neither the Ministry nor the Government of Delhi talked about it and conveniently put it into cold storage. I wondered why such a valuable report was being allowed to die an unusual death and why should the government make such a heavy infructuous expenditure. I learned the hard way that the governments were not willing to take any unpopular decision which has an impact on population growth or on the interests of any group of people, particularly the migrants.

Meanwhile, with its burgeoning population, uncontrollable pollution, unchecked growth of slums, inhuman transport system, lack of basic amenities to large sections of the population, chaotic traffic, garbage and dirt, resurfacing of diseases of all kinds and degenerated municipal services, Delhi inevitably marched towards getting the dubious distinction of being labelled as one of the worst cities in the world.

IX

Tajmahal Turning Saffron!

One day, the Ministry of Environment woke up with the disturbing news that Tajmahal had lost its shining whiteness and had turned yellow. It was also reported that emissions from the Mathura petroleum refinery were responsible for discolouring the Taj. The Ministry being far removed from reality as usual was not at all aware of this damaging development.

Tajmahal has been India's best advertisement to the western world and millions of people come to India to visit Tajmahal and the report would cause incalculable damage to India's tourism. Naturally, the Ministry and in fact, the whole Central Government got worried. The Ministry did, what all ministries do best in such situations, call an inter-ministerial meeting immediately to assess the situation and how best the problem could be tackled. In the meeting, it was decided to appoint a committee of experts headed by Mr. Vardarajan, well-known scientist and Director-General of CSIR to look into the problems associated with this phenomenon and also to suggest remedial measures.

The Vardarajan Committee took more than one year to submit its report to the Ministry. They visited Mathura and Agra several times making on-the-spot study of all the technical parameters in the suspected industrial establishments. The committee submitted a highly technical report coming to the conclusion that the Mathura Refinery was not responsible for making the Taj yellow and the culprits were the foundries near the Taj emitting toxic fumes which settled on the Taj domes and minars. The committee also suggested closing of all foundries within a 5- kilometre zone and resettle them outside the zone. As for the Mathura Refinery, there was no radical recommendation either for possible shifting of the refinery or to change the existing technologies used by the refinery.

Mr. Vardarajan based his conclusions on detailed analysis of a number of technical data like the composition of the chemicals present in the emissions of the refinery, the distance to which the pollutants could travel and the pattern of wind direction from the refinery to the Taj. The distance between the refinery and the Taj was more than 50 kilometres and the pollutant particles, argued Mr. Vardarajan, could not have reached the Taj; the pollutants moved up and down in waves along the wind movement and totally dissipated before they could touch the Taj. Therefore, it is the nearby foundries of Agra which were causing damage to the Taj giving it the yellow colour.

The report surprised many in the ministry including me. But, the problem was if there is a technical report by an eminent scientist, it cannot be contested by any generalist whatever his experience could be. It could be relooked by another scientist or expert who had a higher standing or by a foreign expert of any standing. Most of the senior administrators in the Ministry firmly believed that the Mathura Refinery was definitely responsible for the deterioration of the Taj. I also felt that the refinery must have been somehow affecting the Taj. Foundries in Agra had been there for ages, much before the refinery was built. There could have some additions to the number but the quantum of their emissions and the ashes could not have an impact on a massive scale as to directly discolour the Taj. Secondly, the yellow deposits on the Taj are oily and sticky special to petroleum products and the emissions of the foundries should have given a smoky or black look and not a yellow coating. The suspicion was that the micro particles of the refinery emissions must be surviving in the atmosphere after dissipation and slowly collecting on the marbles. But the administrators' common sense approach did have no meaning in the given situation.

Therefore, nothing was done. The foundries could not be shifted en-mass because of many reasons including political. The Mathura Refinery merrily went on emitting its pollutants and the Taj continued to turn yellow every year. The institution which faced the music was the Archaeological Survey of India which has to undertake every year the gigantic task of cleaning and washing of the Taj at considerable public expenditure to bring back its old glory.

Chapter Four

Democracy Or Demockery!

I

Who Asks The Parliament Questions!

Whether our MPs are the real authors of the Parliament Questions and how many MPs take pains to frame the questions themselves or are serious in getting honest answers from the government was a tricky question which was difficult to answer. But the general perception in the Central Ministries had been that most of the Parliament Questions were motivated. The 'Unstarred Questions' did not bother the government because the replies were laid on the Table of the House and no further explanation was required. It is the 'Starred Question' which bothers the government because the MP has to ask the question himself and the Minister in charge has to reply in person not only the question but also the supplementary questions and if the Minister's reply is not satisfactory, he has to give an 'Assurance' and submit a detailed report to the House within six months. There were enough rumours on the corridors that if someone was interested in raising an issue in the Parliament he can always find some MPs who would oblige him for a consideration. 'Cash for Question' had been an open secret and became a standard practice with some MPs. The *modus operandi* had been that a Personal Assistant will be in possession of the MP's letterhead pad and would give the blank letterhead to you for a consideration and what you have to do is to type out the question and hand over the paper to the Personal Assistant who would get the signature of the MP and would cause it to be submitted to the Question Division of the Lok Sabha or the Rajya Sabha Secretariat as the case may be. The rumour about the consideration had been Rs.5000 for an Unstarred Question and Rs. 10,000 for a Starred Question but there was no guarantee that the Questions would be selected for oral answer or written reply. The rot in the system had never been discussed in Parliament (although everybody knew about it) because there could be no direct proof of the transactions.

The Indian Parliament since independence had devised a time tested system of filtering the questions through the institution of Examiner, Questions in the Lok Sabha and Rajya Sabha Secretariats. All questions which did not meet the parliamentary standards and which were not in the interest of the security, unity and integrity of the nation were weeded out and never admitted by the Speaker. The system served the Parliament well for almost four decades. With fast deteriorating standards of Parliamentary functioning and marked qualitative changes in the profiles of the MPs, the importance and dignity of the Question Hour suffered a set-back. On the plea that the majority of the MPs did not get an opportunity of being heard and only the questions raised by a few elite MPs were being admitted, pressures were mounted on the Speaker, Lok Sabha and the Chairman, Rajya Sabha to scrap the office of the Examiner, Questions. Sometime in 1990s, the system of filtering Parliament Questions was replaced by a system of selection by lottery, which seemed to many an absurd system pregnant with triviality and non-seriousness.

I was one of the victims of the new system. *Kendriya Bhandar* was flooded with parliament questions, both starred and un-starred. While in the past, there had hardly been any Parliament question against a cooperative organisation like Kendriya Bhandar, it was surprising that it received half a dozen questions every week during my tenure. Even the Minister thought there must have been something seriously wrong with the management of Kendriya Bhandar. Most of the questions were silly and personal attacks on the Chairman and not on the performance of the organisation.

The sudden love for *Kendriya Bhandar* of a group of MPs, though intriguing, was not entirely unwelcome because it received considerable publicity and undue public attention. But when the spate of questions went on unabated, we started enquiring where we had gone wrong and what could be the real motives behind these questions. Our investigations revealed that a few suppliers who were deregistered or blacklisted by us because either they were fake or involved in frauds, were generating these questions though some of the MPs who had unholy connections with them. It was also found that only a few MPs belonging to a particular political party of Bihar known for their muscle power were asking the questions. Knowing the background of these MPs, we got a doubt whether these MPs on whose names the questions were being raised were the actual authors of the questions. One day, I told my General Manager Sudarshan 'let us meet and discuss these questions with these MPs; I am sure they may not be aware that they raised so many repetitive questions.' So, an appointment was fixed with a very prominent and vocal MP of Bihar, who belonged to a regional Party well-known for their money and muscle power. This party was the ruling Party in Bihar but was in the opposition bench in the Parliament. Normally, Members belonging to the ruling Party or the ruling Coalition restrain themselves from asking uncomfortable or irresponsible questions to embarrass the government; the 'missiles' come mainly from the opposition bench.

There was one hitch about the meeting- what should be the venue of the meeting. The MP wanted to meet us at his official bungalow at Talkatora Road. On my own, I had never tried to meet an MP or a politician, not to speak of going over to their residences during my entire tenure in the Central Secretariat- I always kept a safe distance from the politicians. But in this case, I could not avoid the embarrassment since I had already committed to the meeting. So, on the appointed day, I proceeded to the bungalow of the MP without my General Manager who excused himself at the last moment (very clever of him!). I was made to wait for more than half an hour in his office room and then the MP himself came and guided me to an inner room and I was in for a shock – the supplier whom I had blacklisted was sitting in the room. When asked why he was there, the MP explained that he had been working as one of his assistants and that he had been taking care of his typing work. Now, I could understand the source of the continuous flow of Parliament questions on purchase and supply of materials. Without much formality, I started the drama by praising the MP's oratorical powers and the important position he holds in the Parliament and the need to hold the dignity he commands. I said 'Sir, I am sure you will not certainly like to see your high reputation to be sullied by silly questions attributed to you! I cannot believe that you have signed these questions; somebody is misusing your position'. I took out of my bag a dozen selected questions and showed them to him. He had close look at the questions and admitted very frankly 'yes, I have signed one or two questions but not all of them'. Obviously, his stenographer (the blacklisted supplier) impersonated him and having got a typewriter was making full use of it to promote his case by maligning Kendriya Bhandar. The MP was crude enough to suggest that this would stop but I must take care of the blacklisted supplier who was found during inspection not having an establishment and had been working with a false address. I thanked the MP saying that 'I would certainly look into this but the MP would certainly not ask me to do anything illegal'.

From that day onwards, there was no further embarrassing questions from this particular MP. We heaved a sigh of relief. Needless to say, I did nothing to rehabilitate the rogue supplier. This is an example of gross misuse of Parliamentary questions and how the MPs are taken for a ride.

II

Who is Afraid of the CBI?

The Central Bureau of Investigation (CBI) had been created with high hopes that one day India could become a corruption-free nation. Like all other countries in the world, corruption had been a part of life for the Indians from time immemorial. The British Administration must be credited for the establishment of steel -frame bureaucracy which functioned with ruthlessness for about two hundred years making the higher bureaucracy and the higher judiciary corruption-free. The common perception during the British days and even after independence had been that the ICS officers and the judges of the High Courts and the Supreme Court were incorruptible. But the same perception was not there for the lower bureaucracy which was riddled with corruption. Corruption at the lower levels had always been rampant so much so that the entire Indian society accepted it as normal. No shame was attached to matrimonial advertisements in the newspapers declaring how much the prospective bridegroom was earning as "extra income" in addition to his regular salary. The citizens were reconciled to the fact that they had to pay a certain amount of bribe to get their things done and it became a part of life. They even did not grudge paying the small ticket bribes to their Indian brothers working under the colonial government because their main grudge was living in indignity, almost like slaves, under the British rule. Therefore, the wings of the government merrily 'adopted' small time corruption as part of their functioning and 'systematized' the system of payments fixing the percentage admissible to the various levels of functionaries. Most prominent among the departments were the Police, the Registration Office, the Railways, the Collectorate, the lower Judiciary and the Public Works Department (PWD). The PWD had gone to the extreme of issuing unofficial circulars fixing varying percentages of the contract value, which should be admissible to the Accounts staff, the Assistant Engineer, the Executive Engineer and the Superintendent Engineer. Many years later, while dealing with the engineering departments, I came across similar circulars but the only difference was officials of higher rank like that of Chief engineer and Engineer-in Chief were brought under the ambit. The funniest thing I found in these departments was that definition of honesty. Those officials or Engineers who never questioned or created any controversy about the quantum of bribe contained in the 'special envelops' delivered to them and who kept the envelope quietly without bothering to count were considered most 'honest'.

Therefore, the British Administration was functioning smoothly with this small ticket corruption and since it did not hurt the citizens who took it as part of their daily life, there were no debates or public awareness about corruption in British Administration. Another reason had been that the citizens did not have the liberty to question the honesty of the Colonial Administration because the His Majesty's Government could do no wrong. The British administration did nothing to prevent corruption at the lower levels of bureaucracy. On the other hand, it had a tacit support for it and turned a blind eye to this phenomenon. It was a premeditated and a deliberate decision not to disturb a system developed over years under the rule of the East India Company. It would require setting up of a vast machinery to keep watch over a large number of officials at various levels. Moreover, any dismissal or disciplinary action against the local Indians would invite unpopularity of the British Raj and was likely to add fuel to the fire of discontent of the nationalist movement. The Englishmen had an extremely poor view of the morality of the average Indians. They assumed that Indians by nature were immoral and corrupt and could not be fully trusted upon. This perception had been responsible for pegging the wages of the lower bureaucracy at an extremely low level, much lower than the subsistence wage in contemporary Britain while keeping salaries of the higher bureaucracy at a much higher level than their counterparts were getting in England. As for example, the view was: the Police Constable would in any case earn a lot of extra income in terms of bribery, so why increase his basic salary at the expense of His Majesty's Government?

The situation in the 500 princely states was far worse than 'British India' in matters of corruption and dishonesty. Excepting a few progressive Princely states, the majority of the princely states had a very poor record of good administration, ethics in governance and economic development. Unmindful of the welfare of the common citizens, those Rajas and Nawabs played dice with administration and were more engrossed in their personal wealth and pleasures, luxuries, hunting, harems and prodigal living in foreign lands. Political morality, social morality and personal morality were at their lowest; therefore, corruption was not an issue at all.

During the entire period of the British rule, the Colonial Administration took ample measures to ensure that the image of His Majesty's Government was not sullied and therefore, saw to it that corruption did not creep in the higher Bureaucracy, the higher Judiciary and the and Council Members. One of the most distinguishing features of British Administration had been that it did not allow corporate corruption, political corruption and bureaucratic corruption at higher places to take roots in India, which became deep-rooted later in independent India.

In all countries, the corporates become the fountain-head of corruption. Political corruption starts with election politics requiring enormous amount of funds which are mainly provided by the business houses. No big business can be run without political support and friendly economic policies. Sometimes coerced, sometimes for getting favours and sometimes to make political friends, some of the business houses are involuntarily drawn into the circle of political-police-criminal nexus and having entered the unholy muddy water, they cannot come out unscathed; more often than not, they are sucked into the political whirlpool.

Political corruption grew like the 'Frankenstein Monster' with the introduction of the Five-Year Plans which envisaged massive public expenditure in all sectors of the economy opening the floodgates of corruption. The Five Year Plans provided the politicians with the proverbial 'Aladdin's Lamp' with which they invoked the Genie of corruption to deliver anything they wanted to have. Sizable portions of billions of dollars spent on infrastructure projects, Defence, development schemes, rural development and the public sector undertakings found their way to the politicians, the contractors and the bureaucrats. A part of this money filled the coffers of the political parties who did not shy away from spending millions of rupees in election battles. The game of politics became the most profitable business which thrived on money power, muscle power and the power of unscrupulousness, arrogance, ignorance and disrespect. There was a beeline of youths who could do nothing in life for joining politics and make a good harvest. Politics became a gamble, as well-organized as casinos, and if you could throw your dice correctly, you could be millionaire in no time. The corrupt, the criminals and the self-seekers swelled the ranks of political parties. In the Thirteenth Lok Sabha, 162 members of Parliament constituting nearly $1/3^{rd}$ of the House were reported to have criminal records and some of them were accused of heinous crimes. Can these lawmakers be expected to defend and protect the Constitution of India, the Parliament of India and the lives of the citizens of India? Worse has been the situation in the states where the Legislative Assemblies are more unruly stuffed with more musclemen.

It is a sort of Greek tragedy that the loftiest Constitution of the world ushering in a most liberal democracy should pave the way for the corrupt and the criminals to occupy the seats of most sacred institution of Parliament and there was no serious will to prevent it. One institution which could probably make a difference in the matter of cleaning public life was the Central Bureau of Investigation.

The Central Bureau of Investigation (CBI) was created in 1963 by a Resolution of the Home Ministry. It owes its origin to the *Special Police Establishment* set up in 1941 by the Government of India to investigate war-time corruption but its powers and jurisdictions were widened from time to time to cover new areas. Gradually, CBI became the 'premier investigating police agency in India and an elite force which plays a major role in the preservation of values in public life and ensuring the health of national economy'. The services of its investigating officers are sought for all serious criminal probes. The CBI is the official Interpol unit for India. Its motto is "*Industry, Impartiality, and Integrity*". While analogous in structure to the FBI the CBI's powers and functions are severely limited to specific crimes based on the *Delhi Special Police Establishment Act, 1946.*

Questions have been raised again and again about the autonomy of the CBI *vis-a-vis* the government and how much independence the CBI enjoys in their day-to-day functioning of deciding and conducting investigations against corruption. The Central Government have always claimed that it is independent of the government and it never interferes in the investigation process while the CBI Directors come up with the contradictory statement that it is an organ working as part of the government under the supervision of the Central Government.

The debate is meaningless if we consider the circumstances under which the CBI functions. The CBI is controlled by the Ministry of Personnel, Administrative Reforms and Pensions of which the Prime Minister is the Minister in charge. It has been the long-standing practice since Independence that the Director, Intelligence Bureau (IB) and Director, CBI would meet the Prime Minister every week for a weekly review of things and taking stock of the security situation and in the process, they get enough orders or hints about how to carry out their duties. Secondly, there is no Act or Law granting autonomy or independence to

CBI's functioning. Thirdly, there is a rule that the CBI has to obtain written approval of the government at the highest level that is, the Prime Minister before the CBI can initiate a process of investigation against an officer of the rank of Joint Secretary and above and against any minister and political bigwigs. This particular rule virtually paralysed the CBI's functions. Firstly, permission is never given on time to start investigation against senior officers, ministers and politicians and if given at all, they are subsequently withdrawn. I know of many cases where serious charges against IAS officers were dropped one by one by the CBI under pressure from the Personnel Secretary. Secondly, the system does not allow the CBI to start *suo motto* investigation into areas where they think serious corruption or fraud has taken place; they have to wait for signals or requests from the governments. Generally, the investigations sponsored and supervised by the government produced shoddy reports which could not be enforced in the courts of law and did not lead to convictions of the big culprits. That is why the Supreme Court stepped in and introduced a new mechanism of CBI investigations under the Court's supervision by constituting a Special Investigation Team (SIT) in very serious cases. This cast serious aspersions on the credibility of the government and the neutrality of the CBI itself.

To describe CBI as the 'lapdog' of the government is to give some credit to the organisation; it is worse than that. At least the lapdog can bark at its will to drive away intruders or if it notices anything unusual, but the CBI cannot even bark without the permission of the government. Senior officers of the CBI have abrogated their rights and duties to their political bosses; they conveniently forget that their allegiance has to be to the laws of the country and the Constitution and not to political parties. Sadly, the honest officers are demoralised, humiliated and punished for not toeing the official line. The officers who compromise and help the political bosses are rewarded. Otherwise, how do you explain the CBI and IB Directors getting plump postings after retirement including the prestigious post of Governors of Indian States?

No doubt, the CBI is a specialist organisation consisting of experienced, motivated and capable officers and they have shown outstanding results in investigations where they have been given a free hand and where the government did not have any stake to grind. But, the fact remains that the CBI has been used and it has obediently acted as the instrument of political suppression and political vendetta, mainly for the political opponents. It started long ago by Mrs. Gandhi who used IB, RAW and the CBI to prepare dossiers for political personalities including her own party colleagues. She ruled with an iron hand taking a cue from the British Iron Lady, Mrs. Thatcher but, as far as I know, Mrs. Thatcher never used British

Intelligence to 'fix' her opponents. Mrs. Gandhi could control any dissidence anywhere within her own party using the dossiers carefully compiled and updated by the intelligence agencies in the same manner as were maintained for the bureaucrats.

It would not perhaps be an overstatement if one says that no important politician or a senior bureaucrat has gone to jail because of CBI's own efforts to prosecute and convict the culprits bringing their investigations to a logical conclusion through the courts following the normal procedure. Whatever prosecutions and convictions which have taken place for important people is entirely due to the direct intervention of the highest Court of the country, which had to bring the CBI under their direct control and supervision for a fair and impartial investigation in these cases.

In 1987, the Swedish radio alleged that AB Bofors clinched the 55mm Howitzer gun deal by paying bribes to the top Indian politicians and defence officials. It was left to Chitra Subramanian, a young journalist based in Geneva to create a sensation by obtaining 350 documents from the Swedish authorities and despatch one after another the unbelievable stories with documentary proofs to *The Hindu* which published them. After publishing a few stories, *The Hindu* suddenly stopped publishing her further despatches. N. Ram collaborated with Subramanian to reach great heights in investigative journalism but had to stop midway under tremendous political pressures. She then approached *The Indian Express* and *The Statesman*, known for their fearless independence, who agreed to publish all her despatches. Despite N. Ram's unfortunate episode with *The Hindu*, the Bofors story authored by Subramanian and Ram was adjudged by Columbia University's School of Journalism as one of the 50 best stories since 1915.

Chitra Subramanian's stories based on 350 leaked Swedish documents proved that the kickbacks had been paid to the Indian politicians and although they failed to prove involvement of Rajiv Gandhi, all fingers pointed to a certain person close to the Gandhi family. Interestingly, the whistleblower who leaked the Swedish documents to Subramanian was none other than Sten Lindstrom, the former Swedish Police Chief, and an outstanding officer of high repute.

The Comptroller & Auditor general of India tabled a report on the Bofors deal in 1989, which created great uproar and turmoil in the Parliament. The Report squarely indicted Rajiv Gandhi government. The government was forced to constitute a Joint Parliamentary Committee to investigate into the allegations of kickbacks and other irregularities under the chairmanship of B. Shankaranand. Nothing came out of the Joint Parliamentary Committee proceedings as had been the history of such committees. Meanwhile, amid allegations and counter-allegations and difference of opinion on the question of cancelling the deal, there had been a spate of resignations, first by Arun Singh and then V.P. Singh. It is believed that the CAG's report was instrumental in causing the fall of Rajiv Gandhi government. But, it must be recognized that Chitra Subramanian's incisive investigations which directly proved the link between the kickbacks and the Indian politicians and the middleman, Quattrocchi had greater contribution for the downfall of Rajiv Gandhi.

The CBI was sandwiched between the Congress-led and the NDA- led governments. Between 1987 when the Bofors bribery scandal broke out and 1999 when Atal Behari Vajpayee became the prime Minister, for long 12 years, the CBI did practically nothing except to try to 'protect' 'somebody'. In 1997, after a long legal battle, the Swedish bank released 500 documents and CBI was directed to file charge sheet against the culprits, which the CBI did in 1999. The charge sheet was filed in Delhi High Court against Quattrocchi, Win Chadha, Rajiv Gandhi, S.K.Bhatnagar (former Defence Secretary) and others. Towards the end of 2001, Win Chadha and S. K. Bhatnagar died. In June 2002, the High Court quashed all the proceedings but the Supreme Court upheld the CBI's charge sheet in July 2003.

In 2004, the Congress party came to power again and one of the first things they did was to undertake a massive cover-up operation using the CBI. In May 2005, the Delhi Court quashed all bribery charges against Rajiv Gandhi and others. In December 2005, India's Solicitor General requested the British Government to defreeze Quattrocchi's two bank accounts which remained frozen during NDA regime. In January 2006, the Supreme Court directed the government to ensure that no money was withdrawn from these two accounts. The CBI intimated the Supreme Court that Quattrocchi had already withdrawn $6.5 million from this accounts. This meant that Quattrocchi was allowed to withdraw the entire money from these accounts leaving only a statutory minimum balance. But, nobody questioned wherefrom did Quattrocchi get such a huge amount and whereto did he transfer these funds?

The cat and mouse game played between Quattrocchi and the CBI is very interesting - the clever friendly cat will never catch the mouse and pretending to catch it will always leave an escape route for the mouse to fool the cat! In January 2007, the CBI filed an affidavit to the Supreme Court that they were still pursing Quattrocchi's extradition to India and that the *Interpol* had a long-standing red corner notice to arrest Quattrocchi. It is a sad commentary on the CBI that they misled the highest court of the country and the people of India knowing full well that they were not serious about it and they would follow the instructions of their political bosses not to extradite Quattrocchi to India.

A question which has never been asked who would be accountable for CBI's spending so much of public money and making a record number of round the world trips to "catch" Quattrocchi? First, it was in Malaysia where a well-rehearsed drama was staged. The CBI announced that Quattrocchi had been found in Kuala Lumpur and that the CBI was sure to arrest him and bring him to India. The whole nation believed it. But the CBI came back empty-handed blaming non-cooperation from the Malaysian Government which allowed Quattrocchi to quietly slip out of Malaysia for unknown destination long before the CBI team reached Kuala Lumpur.

Thereafter, Quattrocchi surfaced in various parts of the world but before CBI could reach him, he would receive advance information and would shift his base to another country. This went on till 2011 when CBI disclosed that Quattrocchi had been detained in Argentina, 15 days after detention by the Argentine police. This time, the CBI was ready to launch a final 'assault' to catch the big fish with a jumbo team consisting of police sleuths, lawyers and translators. And a bigger drama was enacted. There was no extradition treaty between India and Argentina. In this situation the basic document which was required to be produced along with the request for extradition was a valid court order for arrest. The big Indian delegation did not carry any. Did they not know that this was the basic requirement? So, was it not done deliberately? The inevitable happened. The Argentine court rejected Indian request for arrest on the simple reason that India could not produce any valid court order for arrest. And Quattrocchi was set free. Quattrocchi became a free man in March 2011 when a Delhi Court did not find sufficient evidence against him. In July, 2013, Quattrocchi died of heart attack at Milan. But, the case is going on!

My reading of the case is that Quattrocchi would have done well and lived longer had he decided to face the Indian courts (which are most liberal as compared to US or European courts) declaring that he did receive the commission for the services he rendered as an agent. Accepting commission for the services of an agent is a valid payment and he could have fought it out. The only people who would have been grossly embarrassed were Bofors, the Swedish and the Indian Governments because they declared that there was no agent in the deal and that no commission had been paid to any agent. It appears Quattrocchi was prevented from doing so by the powerful people surrounding him, who feared the exposure.

The CBI has been brutally criticised (partly unfairly) by politicians, civil societies, the media and the people at large for its deliberate failure attributable to its delay in lodging FIR, delay in sending letter *rogatories*, not appealing against Delhi High Court order of 2004, de-freezing Quattrocchi's London accounts, putting up a very weak case for extradition from Argentina, withdrawal of Interpol Red Corner notice and final withdrawal of the case against Quattrocchi. The Chief Metropolitan Magistrate (Vinod Yadav) could not help commenting *"I agree that there are certain malafide intentions in the case and there is no doubt in that"*.

In many ways, Bofors scandal remains one of the biggest scandals in Indian history although the amount of bribe was only Rs 64 crore. But the CBI created for itself a bigger scandal by spending a whopping amount of Rs.250 crore on the case much of which was spent on infructuous foreign jaunts. Who would be made accountable for this?

The list of CBI's 'deliberate failures' and playing political games at the behest of the ruling party is rather long. Whether it the Fodder Scam of Lalu Yadav or the Disproportionate Assets (DR) cases against Mulayam Singh or Mayawati, the pattern is the same; the cases are kept in the backburner and are used by the ruling party whenever they wish to tighten the screw. The CBI has been used by all governments to win political battles with their adversaries.

III

Cows Laid Golden Eggs in Bihar!

The Fodder Scam which occurred in the poor state of Bihar is a very serious corruption case in which the involvement of the then Chief Minister of Bihar was crystal clear as evidenced by the report of the Comptroller and Auditor general of India and the investigations made by the Joint Director of CBI, Eastern Region. The joint Director who framed charge sheet against Chief Minister (CM) and wanted to file it in the court of law was unceremoniously removed from his responsibilities and humiliated.

The fodder scam is no less thrilling than the 'Great Train Robbery'; it was a broad day-light robbery of creatures who could not speak – the cows and buffalos. Nobody heard of cows laying golden eggs but they did in Bihar! Depriving the cows and buffalos of their medicines and fodder, it was a free looting of the Bihar Treasuries by producing false bills, which continued for years and in which a number of politicians and senior officials were involved including Chief Ministers. I think such a blatant, brazen and daring theft of public funds had never taken place in the civilized world.

It is a long story. It was in 1985 when the CAG of India and the AG of Bihar noticed large scale irregularities in Bihar Treasuries and warned the

Bihar Government. But the warnings were not heeded by successive governments. In 1992, Bidhu Bhusan Dwivedi, a Police Inspector in the Anti- Corruption Unit, in a report sent to the Inspector General of the Vigilance Department revealed for the first time the existence of a fodder scam and the possible involvement of the Chief Ministers. Dwivedi was immediately transferred out of the Anti- corruption unit and suspended from the post (his honour restored by the Jharkhand High Court and taken as witness later). In January 1996, Amit Khera, Deputy Commissioner of West Singbhum district showed exemplary courage in conducting raids to the Animal Husbandry department in Chaibasa town and the seized documents indicated large-scale embezzlements by an organised mafia of officials and business people. His report did not mention Lalu or other politicians. The story broke and the country was shocked. As a measure of cover-up, the CM immediately constituted a committee of officials to inquire into the allegations. But, the voices demanding a CBI probe became louder and louder. It was because of a Public Litigation Petition in the Supreme Court that the investigation could be seriously started. The Supreme Court directed the Patna High Court to hand over the case to the CBI which was done in March 1996. In 1997, the CBI team was headed by the Joint Director, U. N. Biswas unearthed direct linkages of the ruling Chief Minister. In May 1997, the CBI requested the Governor of Bihar, A.R.Kidwai to grant permission to prosecute the CM and others. In June, 1997, the CBI filed charge sheets against the CM and 55 other co-accused. The CM used his influence to bring a privilege motion against U.N.Biswas who had to tender unconditional apology for his behaviour. Later, U.N. Biswas was further humiliated (for his good work!) when he was transferred and relieved of his post as the principal investigating officer in the case. Obviously, the politicians sensed victory.

The same thing happened to the reports of the CAG, which conclusively proved that there been fraudulent withdrawal of government funds of about 9.5 billion rupees (US$160 million) in the Animal Husbandry Department for supply of fodder and medicines which never arrived. The CAG reports were never discussed in the Public Accounts Committee of Bihar Assembly. On the other hand, the CM showed his power by issuing summons to the Accountant General (AG) to appear before the Assembly for explanation (for writing such reports). The AG was also receiving numerous calls threatening him and his family, for which he had to seek 24-hour police protection. Two developments saved the life of the AG. The CAG took up the matter with the Central Government saying that the AG had been his Representative in the States and therefore, he cannot be summoned by the State of Bihar. The Central Government agreed with his position that as part of a Constitutional Authority, the AG cannot be summoned by the Bihar Assembly because one Constitutional body cannot encroach upon the functions of another Constitutional body. Another coincidence was the Police Commissioner happened to be Sikh gentleman of high integrity and he assured full safety to the AG and his family.

In a related case of disproportionate income (DA), in 1998, the Income Tax Department claimed that the CM made Rs.4.6 million from the fodder scandal. The CM and his wife were charge - sheeted but in April 2000, they were acquitted of the charges by the special CBI court. The CBI this time did not appeal against the verdict. The Government of Bihar challenged the verdict in Patna High Court which accepted the plea. But, the CM and the CBI both challenged the ruling in the Supreme Court. However, in various twists and turns, the CM and his wife got relief from the Supreme Court till 2012 when the Supreme Court had agreed to review its own ruling.

The Fodder Scam or *Chara Ghotala* involved embezzlement of tax-payers money to the tune of Rs.9.6 billion (Rs. 20 billion or $350million at 2013price level). Till May 2013, trials in 44 cases out 53 cases were complete and punishments ranging from 2 years to 7 years had been handed down by the courts. Interestingly, in one of the cases, 20 truckloads of documents were produced before the Court at Ranchi. More than 500 people were convicted; most prominent among them had been R.K. Rana, Member of Parliament and Dhruv Bhagat, former Member of Legislative Assembly. It is not known if the courts had ordered recovery of the stolen money or confiscation of their properties. But the most important politician involved in the scam was roaming free and was playing a leading role in national politics being an ally of the Congress party and a vocal Member of the Lok Sabha. Except for sporadic police remand and a short stint in jail he had presided over the Government of Bihar for more than 10 years during which a reign of terror and *jungle raj* was unleashed. He won elections after elections and finally came to the Lok Sabha after his party lost power in Bihar to a rival party. In March 2012, 16 years after CBI started investigations, a special CBI court in Patna framed charges against the former Chief Ministers and 32 other accused. During the intervening period, six accused died, two accused turned approvers and two others evaded arrest. Finally, a trial Court at Ranchi found the ex-CM guilty of committing the Fodder Scam and sentenced him to five years of jail term. But he went on Appeal to the High Court which granted him bail till his final conviction. Nobody has heard about the case since then and the politician was again active in politics and was the major factor in bringing his party to power in Bihar in collaboration with his former bitter rival party. The only redeeming feature in the episode has been that the Supreme Court debarred him from contesting elections for six years and he had to vacate his Parliamentary seat following this verdict.

In this case, one of the CBI Directors, Joginder Singh showed considerable independence when he proceeded to prosecute the CM without consulting the then Prime Minister, I.K.Gujral who was dependent on the support of this politician. Joginder Singh alleged that I.K.Gujral tried to block prosecution. But, earlier he received support from the former Prime Minister H.D.Deve Gowda who was a friend of the accused but fell out on certain issues. Later developments did not cover the CBI with glory; they became a party to the delaying tactics and played to the tunes of the party in power.

No finality has been achieved for this harrowing scam even after 27 years! Had it occurred in the United States, justice would have been delivered probably within six months and all accused would have been in jail ranging from 10 years to 50 years. Bernard Madoff, former Chairman of NASDAQ got 125 years of imprisonment for a Ponzi scheme for cheating the investors. India has not heard of such harsh punishments. It is a sad commentary on the investigating agencies and the legal system of the country that the rich and the powerful always get the protection of law. The lawyers ingenuously exploit the loopholes in the legal system to delay justice for years and in some cases for decades; the victims and the common people can never expect quick justice. What happened in Bihar was nothing but murder of democracy but public memory is so short that the voters forget everything and elect the same corrupt and tainted politicians again and again as their saviours.

IV

Is India a Republic of Scams?

Corruption has always been a part of life in India. In fact, no country in the world is immune to corruption but it is seen more pronounced in India because of its socio-cultural milieu owing to historical reasons. Overt and covert corrupt practices were built in the administrative system during the colonial rule and these petty corruptions were not considered as sins. After Independence, political corruption, business corruption, black money generation and political-criminal nexus added new dimensions to the corruption scenario in India, which had the effect of making India as one the most corrupt countries in the world.

According to Transparency International's Corruption Perception Index, India ranked 94th (2012) out of 176 countries tied with Benin, Colombia, Djibouti, Greece, Moldova, Mongolia, and Senegal. In a study conducted by Transparency International in

2008, it was found that 40% of Indians had firsthand experience of paying bribes or using a contact to get a job done in public office.

By western standard, India has always been a corrupt country. But the rate of occurrence and the magnitudes of political corruption siphoning off billions of dollars of public funds have perhaps surpassed all other countries of the world. According to an estimate made by Swiss Banks Association (which they later denied), the amount of black money stashed by Indians in foreign banks would have exceeded the black monies of all other countries of the world put together. Starting from the Jeep Scandal in 1948 and ending up with the VVIP Chopper Purchase scandal in 2013, there have been at least 200 major and countless minor scandals in India. An early estimate (or guesstimate!) based on pieces of information available with various World bodies and NGOs had put the value of scams committed by various sections of Indians at about Rs.73, 00, 000, 00, 00,000. A more reliable estimate made recently by three economists of the Bank of Italy has come out with a figure of about seven trillion US dollars of the black money stacked in the tax havens of the world. Gabriel Zucman of the London School of Economics estimated the amount of black wealth in tax havens at $7.6 trillion; the Boston Consulting Group put it at $8.9 trillion and the Tax Justice Network came out with a figure of $21 trillion. The share of Indians in the black wealth hidden in the tax havens has been estimated at $181 billion. But this does not include the vast amount of black wealth generated and kept within India. Some of the biggest and unbelievable scandals which shocked the conscience of the nation and put India to shame were:

1948: Jeep Scandal Case – the first major scandal in Independent India, in which V. K. Krishna Menon, the then High Commissioner of India to UK bypassed the protocol to sign a contract worth Rs. 80 lakh (a huge money those days) with a foreign firm for the supply of 4603 jeeps for Indian Army. According to a report of the CAG of India, while the High Commission paid the upfront for 4603 jeeps, just 155 jeeps arrived, which the Government of India was forced to accept. Krishna Menon escaped all inquiries and went on to become Indian Prime Minister Jawaharlal Nehru's trusted ally and India's Defence Minister who, because of his faulty policies and arrogance, was largely responsible for the debacle of the Indian Army in the India- China War, 1962.

1951: The Mundhra Scandal - Rs. 12 million (US$ 200,000). Mundhra is considered as the forerunner of financial scamsters of modern India including Harshad Mehta's Security Scam and Abdul Telgi's Stamps Scam and operated with considerable political connivance. However, unlike in the Mundhra case which was revealed by Feroze Gandhi, the present day governments do not take honest action immediately in appointing competent judges for judicial investigations and public hearings. This lack of transparency had been extremely stark in the public investigation of the Bofors Case, one of India's largest scandals, which involved Feroze Gandhi's son Rajiv Gandhi, the then Prime Minister of India.

1956: BHU Funds Misappropriation –Rs.5 million (US$84,000). 1960: Teja Loan Scandal –Rs. 220 million (US $ 3.5 million)

1970: The Nagarwala Scandal – Rs. 6 million (US$100,000)

1981: The Cement Scam - Rs.300 million (US$5.0 million) in which there was a direct involvement of prominent Congress leader and former Maharashtra Chief Minister, A.R. Antulay. He had to resign from the post of Chief Minister after the Bombay High Court convicted him of extortion charges.

1986: Bihar Fodder Scam - Rs. 950 crore. This is known in India as the mother of all scandals. The Fodder scam had been going on for over two decades under the direct patronage of Bihar Chief Ministers and senior officials before it came to light in 1996 in the town of Chaibasa, Bihar. With fake government sanctions and fabricated bills for livestock fodder, medicines and equipment, funds were withdrawn from various Treasuries of Bihar and embezzled. The total amount of funds thus embezzled by the Animal husbandry Department through this scheme was estimated at Rs. 950 crore. Then chief minister of Bihar, Lalu Prasad Yadav was forced to resign along with former chief minister Jagannath Mishra in the wake of the scandal and subsequently, convicted by the Court. Lalu Prasad Yadav lost his Parliamentary seat as a result of the court order.

1987: Bofors Gun Scandal – Rs.640 million (US$11 million) The Bofors scandal had been a major corruption scandal in India in the 1980s involving the then Prime Minister Rajiv Gandhi and the Italian businessman, Ottavio Quattrocchi who was close to the Gandhi family. Following the submission of the CAG's Audit Report on the scam to the Indian Parliament, Parliamentary proceedings were stalled and finally led to the defeat of the Congress Party led by Rajiv Gandhi in the 1989 General Election. The case came to light first during Vishwanath Pratap Singh's tenure as Defence Minister, when incriminating information about the payment of the kickbacks were revealed through investigative journalism by Chitra Subramanian and N. Ram of *The Hindu.*

The Defence Ministry and AB Bofors, the biggest arms manufacturer of Sweden signed a US$ 1.3 billion deal for supply of 410 numbers 155 mm field howitzer guns and a supply contract almost twice that amount. It was the biggest arms deal ever in Sweden, and money marked for development projects was diverted to secure this contract at any cost by flouting of rules and bypassing of institutions. The Swedish company paid Rs.640 million (US$11 million) in kickbacks to top Indian politicians and key defence officials.

There is a cruel irony in the scam. While the Bofors Scandal had a very sad endings with the deaths of Rajiv Gandhi, Defence Secretary, S. K. Bhatnagar, the middleman, Win Chadha and the Gandhi family friend, Ottavio Quattrocchi, the Bofors Howitzer guns supplied to India had been "damn good guns" and had won the war for India against Pakistan in 1999. Without the Bofors guns, India could have lost the Kargil War.

1990: Airbus Scandal - Indian Airlines signed a Rs 2,000-crore deal with Airbus instead of Boeing, causing a furore after the crash of an Airbus A-320. New planes were grounded, causing IA a weekly loss of Rs 2.5 crore. But, the real reason for selecting Airbus- 320 against the recommendations of the J.R.D.Tata Committee to purchase Boing-767 had been that while Airbus was willing to offer a kickback even up to 10% of the deal,

Boeing Company was prevented by US Law to offer any bribe money for the Boeing aircraft deals. It was alleged that Airbus offered bribes up to 200 crore to the top politicians in India.

1992: The Indian Bank Scandal - Rs.13 billion (US$220 million) 1992: Harshad Mehta Securities Scam – Rs. 50 billion (US$ 880 million).

1996: Fertiliser Import Scam –Rs. 1.33 billion (US$22 million).

2011: 2G Spectrum Scam – The Comptroller & Auditor General of India in his Audit Report estimated a loss of Rs. 1.6 trillion (US $ 26 billion) owing to non-transparent and corrupt methods followed to allocate the 2-G licences, in which the Minister in charge, A. Raja was personally involved. This was one the of biggest scandals occurring in India. The Supreme Court of India held that those allocations were "unconstitutional and arbitrary" and cancelled 122 licences issued by the Ministry. *The Time* magazine put the scam at second place after the *Watergate Scandal* in their list of "Top 10 Abuses of Power".

2011: The Antrix- Deval Deal – Rs. 200,000 crore. The scam involved former ISRO chairman G Madhavan Nair and three other scientists who were responsible for a controversial contract between Antrix Corporation and

Devas Multimedia Private Limited leasing out S-band transponders in two satellites (GSAT6 and GSAT6A) to Devas. A report of the CAG of India report revealed that the Department of Space (DoS) had violated rules and policies for approving the agreement without realizing that benefit would mainly flow to the private party The audit report pegged the loss at Rs200,000 crore. The Department of Space under Madhavan Nair got approvals to build the satellites without disclosing the fact that they were to be utilized primarily for Devas' benefit.

2012: Y. S. Jaganmohan Reddy Disproportionate Asset Case and Andhra Pradesh land Scam – Rs. 1000 billion (US$17 billion). Y.S.Reddy was in jail for 16 months for interrogation in disproportionate asset case.

2012: The Scorpene Submarine Deal (2012) - Rs. 500 crores (about US $10million) were alleged to have been paid to government decision- takers by Thales Company, the makers of the Scorpene Submarine. The Defence Ministry had approved the submarine deal worth Rs 19,000 crore with Thales in October, 2005.

2012: Bellary Mining Scam (2012) – Karnataka Government suffered a loss of 80,085 crore owing to illegal mining of iron ore in Bellary district, in which Chief ministers, Ministers and criminalised businessmen looted nation's precious natural resources.

The indiscriminate mining also brought ecological disaster in the entire belt.

2012: Tetra Truck Scam – Rs.750 crore of Defence funds were siphoned off by Defence officials, agents and middlemen in a Defence contract with the Tetra firm of the Czech Republic for the supply and manufacture of Tetra trucks through BEML.

2012: Granite Scam in Tamil Nadu – illegal quarrying of granite to the extent of Rs. 16,000 crore was carried out in Madurai district with the help of prominent politicians and certain high officials.

2012: The Maharashtra Scheme Irrigation – politicians (Minister of Irrigation named) siphoned off Rs. 720 billion (US$ 12 billion).

2012: Uttar Pradesh NRHM Scam (2012) – Rs. 10,000 crore siphoned off by ruling politicians (two Chief Ministers named) in UP.

2012: Karnataka Wakf Board Land Scam (2012) - The Karnataka State Minorities Commission its report alleged misappropriation of Rs.200,000 crore by the Board Members and politicians in allotment of 27, 00 acres of Wakf land.

2012: DIAL Scam – The CAG of India in an Audit Report estimated a loss of Rs. 1.63 lakh crore (US$ 29.4

billion) to the Indian public and a net gain to DIAL owing to lack of diligence in the agreement between the Airports Authority of India and the Delhi International Airport Limited (a consortium of GMR, German and Malaysian airport holdings) for allotment of 4,800 acres of brown field government land (19 square kilometres) including commercial exploitation of a part of it.

2012: The Coal Allocation Scam or "Coalgate" - The CAG of India in his Audit Report alleged an estimated a loss of Rs. 185,590 crore to the government due to irregular and inefficient allocation of coal block to various parties, mainly political favourites.

2013: NSEL (National Spot Exchange) Scam, Mumbai (2013) – NSEL promoted by Financial Technologies India Ltd and NAFED was involved in a scam estimated at RS. 5,600 crore.

2013: Railway Iron Ore Freight Scam -17000 crores Vodafone Tax Scandal (2013) – involved Rs 11,000-crore tax dispute case in India. There were corruption charges on Kapil Sibal because of Law ministry's U-turn to agree to conciliation in Vodafone tax case.

2013: Sharadha Group Financial Scandal – was a financial scam caused by the collapse of a Pozi Scheme run by Saradha Group (a consortium of over 200 private companies) in West Bengal, Bihar and Orissa and other places of Eastern India. The collapse of the Chit Fund owned by people politically connected with the ruling party in West Bengal caused an estimated loss of R s.200–300 billion (US$4–6 billion) to over 1.7 million depositors.

2013: Kerala Solar Panel Scam - The scam involved a fraudulent Solar Energy company, Team Solar, in Kerala, which used two women to create political contacts with the Ministers and the Chief Minister's office. The masterminds in the scam duped several influential people to the tune of Rs.70 million by offering to make them business partners, or by offering to install solar power units for them and receiving advance payments for the same.

2013: The VVIP Chopper Deal, Chopper Scam or Choppergate – Several Indian politicians and military officials have been accused of accepting bribes from AgustaWestland in order to win the ₹36 billion (US$600 million) Indian contract for the supply of 12 AugustaWestlandAW101 helicopters intended to perform VVIP duties.

2014: Madhya Pradesh State Farmers Welfare and Agriculture Development Minister was involved in a Disproportionate Assets Case - Rs.2000 crores.

2014: Delhi Jal Board Scam (2014) –Rs.10,000 crores.

2014: Hindustan Aeronautics Ltd - Rolls-Royce Defence Scam – Rs.10,000 crores.

2014: Odisha Industrial Land Mortgage Scam - 52,000 crore.

Thus, the list is almost unending. A critical analysis of the trends and patterns of the scams occurring since 1947 reveals certain interesting but disconcerting truths which were in fact dangerous omens for democracy. First, public morality or probity in public life declined very sharply after the 1950s and 1960s and almost vanished after 1980s. Second, major scams occurred at regular intervals after economic liberalization. Contrary to the belief that liberalization would eliminate corruption, liberalization opened up new opportunities for big-ticket corruption. Massive expenditures on rural developments and social welfare measures created gold mines for the politicians and the bureaucrats. Third, no major scam took place without a conspiracy hatched by the politicians and actively aided by the bureaucrats and the businessmen. Fourth, the majority of the scams were perpetrated by a new breed of politicians – the criminal turned politician and businessman turned politician, who entered the parliament and the State legislatures in greater numbers. Finally, it may be noticed that a huge number of big scams took place between 2008 and 2014 when the UPA Government was in power at the Centre.

What had been the role the CBI when the carnage was taking place all over the nation? CBI, not always their own making, played the role of bird watchers to keep the photo-shots in the archives. It became a fat organisation and its expansion was in direct proportion to the increase in scams and corruption cases. But, rate of prosecution declined in direct proportion to the rate of increase in their obesity. Owing to criminalisation of the local police force at many places and above all, their overall ineffectiveness, the local police has lost public trust and therefore, for any serious crime, the clamour has always been to hand over the case to the CBI. At this rate, the country would be left with no credible organization except the CBI to conduct criminal investigation in thousands of cases over the length and breadth of this vast country with 1.25 billion people. It is certainly not fair to ask the CBI to take over each and every serious case where there is a hue and cry or public outrage. The focus of the organisation and its core competence will get lost if they are compelled to spread their energies and activities thin on the ever increasing criminal cases which the local police forces are supposed to investigate and solve.

In spite of the enormous goodwill which still flows for CBI and their unprecedented expansion, the CBI has hardly served the public purpose and has mainly served the political purpose. It has had tremendous capacity to shield or harass politicians or taming them at the right moment. Except in a few cases which are directly monitored by the Supreme Court and the power to give directions have been taken away from the government, the CBI has always acted as a convenient tool in the hands of the ruling political party and has miserably failed to discharge their obligations to the Constitution of India and the people of India. In none of the corruption cases, suo *motto,* the CBI has moved an inch without the direction of the Government or orders received from the Courts of Law. The CBI, the premier investigating and prosecuting agency of the country and political corruption have been allowed to live as strange bedfellows!

V

Where is the LOKPAL (Ombudsman)?

It took nearly two hundred years for the Ombudsman to reach the shores of India from Scandinavia. While the government of Sweden created an Ombudsman for Justice (Justice Ombudsman) in 1809, the Reserve Bank of India prepared a scheme called Banking Ombudsman scheme 1995 and for the first time in India, created the institution of Banking Ombudsman for the Banking Sector under Section 35A of the Banking Regulation Act, 1949. The Banking Ombudsman created at each Regional

Headquarters of RBI effectively started functioning from 1997. The pioneering move of the Reserve Bank provided an opportunity to the Central and State Governments to give momentum to the Ombudsman movement by creating the institution at the Central, State and Local levels to protect citizen's rights and provide better customer services. In the midst of the Governments' lukewarm attitude, the Ombudsman's movement remained a story of unfinished journey and lost opportunities. India is not even a member of the International Council of Ombudsman because India does not have an Ombudsman (i.e. Lokpal) at the national level. According to the International Council of Ombudsman, the role of the Ombudsman is to protect the people against violation of rights, abuse of powers, error, negligence, unfair decisions and maladministration in order to improve public administration and make the government's actions more open and the government and its servants more accountable to members of the public.

In several countries, the office of Ombudsman has been created at the regional, provincial, state and municipal levels of governance. Some countries have Ombudsman offices at the national, regional and sub-national levels, such as Australia, Argentina, Mexico and Spain, while other nations have Ombudsman offices only at the sub-national government level, as in Canada, India and Italy. Public Sector Ombudsman offices are now functional in many countries of Europe, North America, Latin America, the Caribbean, Africa, the Australasia & Pacific Region and Asia.

While Sweden laid the foundation of modern Ombudsman by creating *Justitieombudsmannen* in 1809, the movement did not catch up with other countries until the twentieth century, when it was adopted in other Scandinavian countries - Finland (1919), Denmark (1955) and Norway (1962). The popularity of the Ombudsman's office increased tremendously in the 1960s, as various Commonwealth and other countries (mainly European) established the institution as Alternative Disputes Redressal Mechanism (ADR) like New Zealand (1962), United Kingdom (1967), most Canadian provinces (starting in 1967), Tanzania (1968), Israel (1971), Puerto Rico (1977), Australia (1977 at the federal level), France (1973), Portugal (1975), Austria (1977), Spain (1981), and the Netherlands (1981).

By mid-1983, there were only about twenty-one countries with Ombudsman offices at the provincial/ state or regional levels. However, the transition of many countries to democracy and democratic structures of governance over the past few decades has led to the establishment of many more Ombudsman offices during recent periods. This transition to democracy accompanied by the reform of government, including creation of the Ombudsman and Human Rights offices, has been evident particularly in Latin America, Central and East Europe as well as in parts of Africa and the Asia-Pacific. Countries that have established national Ombudsman offices during this period include Argentina, Costa Rica, Columbia, Guatemala, Peru, Namibia, South Africa, Poland, some francophone African countries, Hungary, Lithuania, Slovenia, the Czech Republic, Thailand and the Philippines.

By 2003, the number of Ombudsman offices increased more than five times to encompass offices both in states with well-established democratic systems and in countries that are younger democracies. Furthermore, the European Union has created a European Ombudsman under the Maastricht Treaty. The first European Ombudsman was appointed in 1995.

In India, the concept of Ombudsman has been implemented in a fragmented and lackadaisical manner. While Lok Ayukts, (a variation of Ombudsman offices) have been appointed in some States, they have hardly been effective and functional in redressal of any kind of public grievances. The Central government has failed to pass the Bill of LOKPAL for more than four decades for the creation of the institution of a Central Ombudsman to deal with complaints of corruption at high places. While the Central Ombudsman scheme has not got off the ground, there has been some progress in certain sectors like Banking, Insurance, and Electricity etc.

The first institution of Ombudsman was created in 1995 when the Reserve Bank of India appointed Banking Ombudsman in a few states. At present, 15 Banking Ombudsmen in various States, each having jurisdiction over one State or a group of States, have been functioning on regional basis for the redressal of all customer complaints in the banking sector. The Banking Ombudsman Scheme has generally been successful in creating awareness among the banks for better customer services and better customer support systems.

Similarly, a number of Insurance Ombudsmen were created in various States covering the whole country to look into the customer complaints against the Insurance Companies. Recently, a number of Electricity Ombudsmen have been appointed for the Power sector under the Energy Act to deal with customers' complaints against the distribution companies. The Ministry of Finance has also constituted Income Tax Ombudsman to look into the grievances of Income Tax payers against the Income Tax Department. It is likely that in future, more and more Ombudsmen will start functioning in various other Sectors like Telecom, Pension, Health, Education etc.

The great advantages of Ombudsman Scheme being purely an Alternative Disputes Redressal Mechanism have been:-

Ombudsman does not follow the lengthy and expensive legal processes and formalities. All complaints receive immediate attention and disputes are resolved through conciliation and consent. Justice is immediate, cost free and hassle free. There is no system of appeals against Ombudsman's order in the Court of law. There is generally full implementation of Ombudsman's orders.

It is a matter of great shame that India, even after 60 years of independence, could not create the institution of Lokpal i.e. the Central Ombudsman. Appointment of the Ombudsman at the national level i.e. Lokpal who will look into corruption at high levels including ministers, legislator and administrators cannot brook further delay. Had there been a Lokpal, India could perhaps have escaped being branded as one of the most corrupt countries in the world. While, the Parliament should immediately enact the long pending Lokpal Bill at the Central level, the States should also initiate a process of creating Rajya Lokpal at the State level to replace the existing Lok Ayukts. Insensible delay and lack of will of successive governments to get the Lokpal bill passed and non-appointment of a Lokpal tantamount to committing a fraud on the people of India because of the inability of the governments to protect the citizens of democratic India from the gross abuse of powers, negligence, unfair decisions, maladministration and corruption. The Ombudsman

Movement in India cannot achieve its objectives and receive international credibility unless the institution is created at the Central, State, Local Government and Public Sector Levels.

VI

Is There Ethics In Governance?

Like *Socialism* in the twentieth century, *Ethics* has been the catchword and the watchword of the twenty-first century. Cutting across nationalities, political, religious and cultural divides, the civil societies all over the world have started questioning the ethicality of government decisions and functioning and in many cases, the very existence of the governance system. Traditional respect for authority has vanished in thin air and has given way to widespread scepticism, mistrust and anger about the real intentions of the people's representatives, the administrators and the police. The people are demanding more transparency, greater openness and greater ethical functioning. People's patience has been tested far too long for tolerating wide-spread corruption, monumental scams, gross misuse of power, dishonesty, unethical activities and criminalities in public life; hence the anger. The 'Arab spring' and Anna Hazare's fight against corruption in India are nothing but manifestations of the same frustration and anger which the common people harbour in almost all countries of the world. The 'trust deficit' between the people and the government and between the people and the corporates has been the consequential off-shoot of wilful violations of the ethical standards.

The concept of ethics owes its origin to the Greek word *Ethos* which means character of an individual or culture of a community. Socrates (469 BC – 399 BC) was the first Greek philosopher who developed the concept of ethics. He tried to encourage both intellectuals and the common citizens to turn their attention from the outside world to the inner world, to the condition of humankind and the welfare of the society. His passion for knowledge and truth made him equate knowledge with virtue and virtue with happiness. A scholar or a wise person will automatically know what is right, will do what is good and will therefore, and be happy. Happiness of the individual as well of the society is the ultimate goal and this goal can be achieved by doing what is right and discarding what is wrong. The Greek philosophers - Socrates, Aristotle, Plato, the Hedonists, the Epicureans, and the Stoics contributed a great deal in the development of ethics in ancient Greece which became the cradle of scientific civilization of the West nurturing many schools of thought in art, culture and philosophy and laid the foundations for the modern social and physical sciences. The Greek philosophers gave to the world the secular principles of ethics for the conduct of individuals and the conduct of rulers.

Great civilizations flourished in the ancient world. Unfortunately, most of the ancient civilizations - the Egyptian, the Mesopotamian, the Babylonian, the Persian, the Mayan, the Assyrian, the Greek and the Roman - were destroyed due to invasions, natural calamities or self-destruction. But the overriding reason for their destruction had been the breakdown of ethical principles of governance on the part of the rulers and the collapse of moral values in the society, weakening the nation and making it a sitting duck for the invaders. The collapse of the Roman Empire was a classic case of a civilization being destroyed by its own internal contradictions. During the rule of Nero (37-67 AD), the last emperor of the Julio-Claudian dynasty, Rome reached its nadir in corruption, conspiracy, immoralities, violence, sexual abuse and a total breakdown of the governance system. The rulers lost all morality to govern inevitably waiting for a catastrophe to happen and destroy the empire.

Two ancient civilizations which have survived the ravages of time as continuing civilizations have been the Chinese and the Indian. These two civilizations survived mainly because of the strong foundations of the society based on high ethical value-systems and strong moral principles. In China, the teachings of Lao Tse and of Confucius became the guiding principles for the kings to rule and for the citizens to lead a good life. Ethical and efficient administration established by the successive Chinese dynasties made a stable, strong and prosperous empire. Similarly, in India, the principles of Karma and Dharma enshrined in the Gita, the teachings of the sages enshrined in the Upanishads and the exemplary models of good rule given by Lord Rama, the Purushottama king in the Ramayana and by king Yudhishtira, the epitome of honesty and truthfulness in the Mahabharata guided all the rulers. During the Buddhist period, the Buddhist kings like Ashoka ruled on the basis of Buddhist principles of non-violence, tolerance, love, selflessness, honesty and ethical economics. It is amazing that a great empire based on non-violence was established from Kandahar to Cambodia and Buddhism as an instrument of governance was embraced from Japan to Sri Lanka.

Therefore, modern ethics including business ethics should have drawn inspiration from the philosophies of these two great civilizations. Instead, modern ethics is entirely based on Western thoughts and- experiences although there is now an increasing realization about the practical applications of the Indian, the Japanese and the Chinese spiritual heritage in modern management.

Modern ethics mainly centres round two moral theories- the *Consequentialist theory* propounded by Jeremy Bentham and John Stuart Mill and the *Non- consequentialist theory* or *Deontological theory* as epitomized by the monumental work of Immanuel Kant's *'A Critique of Pure Reason'*.

Bentham's *Consequentialist theory* or what is known as the *Utilitarian theory* says that any action is moral if the consequence of the action is good and which results in 'maximum good for the maximum number.' The Utilitarian theory also implies 'ends *justify means*'. Mahatma Gandhi, the great crusader of truth and non-violence sternly discarded this theory and said *means are as important as the ends.* The Utilitarian theory does not answer the question 'who benefits'? It does not take into account the possible negative impact which an action may have in terms of environmental degradation, social disparity and discrimination within the target groups.

The non-consequentialist theory or the *Deontological theory*, also known as the *ethic of duty*, says that nothing in this world and indeed, even nothing beyond the world can be conceived which can be called 'good without qualification' except a good will or a sense of duty. Kant argues that to act in the morally right way, people must act from a sense of duty; *it is not the consequences of actions that make them right or wrong but the motives of the person who carries out the action. The highest good must be both good in itself, and good without qualification.* According Kant, those things that are usually thought to be good, such as intelligence, perseverance, hard work etc. fail to be either intrinsically good or good without qualification.

Karl Marx gave a paradigm shift to the concept of morality and ethics and in understanding the individual, the society and the government and their interactions. Pained at unabashed exploitation of the working class and *increasing immiserization of the proletariat* following the industrial revolution, he called for armed revolution against the capitalists, the rich, the exploiters and the ruling class who supported them. Rousseau's slogan *'man is born free, and everywhere he is chains'* was adopted as part of the theory of revolution which justified violence, if required to break the chains for making man free again, as perfectly legitimate and moral.

Post- modern ethics came a long way from the Utilitarian, Deontological and Marxian theories. Post-modern ethics have been shaped by two sets of broad principles – *the Rights Principles and the Justice Principles.* The Rights principles concern various rights which have been nurtured by the United Nations and the international community in general, have been the Human rights, the Democratic rights, Animal Rights, Women's rights, Children's rights, Consumer rights, Right to Information etc. The Justice Principles concern Social Justice- (equality, non-discrimination, and personal freedom), Economic Justice, Environmental Protection, Transparency, Good Governance etc. In earlier era, ethics and moral principles were mainly religion- centric while the present day ethics are based on the *secular principles of Rights and Justice.* In today's world, all ethical questions are to be seen through the lenses of Rights principles and Justice Principles.

Ethics is as old as the ancient civilizations but ethics in management or business ethics is as new as the twenty-first century. It is only in the last decade of the twentieth century and in first decade of the twenty first century that Business Ethics emerged as a separate discipline which has occupied an important place in the Business Schools all over the world starting from Harvard and Wharton.

The industrial revolution which started about 300 years ago and to which the present world belongs, has had four distinct phases:

(a) *Era of Adam Smith –Classical Capitalism and Enlightened self- interest*

(b) *Era of Charles Dickens – Exploitation and Social Injustice*

(c) *Era of Revolution – Marxism, Socialism and Communism*

(d) *Era of Multi-Nationals and Multilateralism*

(e) *Era of Corporate Governance - Corporate Social Responsibility and Ethics in Business and Professions.*

In Adam Smith's world of *Enlightened Capitalism* with free play of market forces, there was no question of interference by the government or the civil society to the unbridled powers of the private enterprises in the conduct of business. Maximization of profits had been the golden principle of business and it was assumed that the profits accruing to the private entrepreneurs would automatically bring prosperity to the society. If the nation's wealth increases, wealth of the citizens would automatically increase. The concept of business ethics was not born.

But the first century of the industrial revolution and unbridled Capitalism witnessed large-scale exploitation of workers and degradation of human dignity as depicted in Charles Dickens' novels. The societies in all the European countries were reeling under extreme greed for profit giving rise to inequalities and social injustice. Adam Smith's world was shattered. The governments were compelled to bring about a large number of legislations on labour relations, minimum wages, and safety of the factories, taxation etc. and a comprehensive Companies Act to regulate every aspect of functioning of the registered companies from their inception to their dissolution – from their birth to death. But there was no awareness of ethics in business.

The Great Depression had come and gone in the thirties. The Second World War devastated the world in the forties. But the War created enormous opportunities for new inventions, innovations and global business. Transnational Companies grew from strength to strength and started controlling international business by producing a major part of world output and through their superior technology; management systems and networking. This gave rise to the oft-quoted *economic imperialism*. It was soon realized that influencing public policies, public finances and public opinion had no longer been the monopoly of the national governments and the transnational corporations (MNCs) were equally powerful in influencing the lives of millions through their products and powers. In fact, the annual income of some of the multinationals was greater than the national income of many sovereign nations in Asia and Africa. Unfortunately, some of them got themselves directly involved in change of regimes and *coup de-tats* in a few Latin American and African countries. Still, there was no debate on ethics in business.

It is only in the early nineties that discussion on business ethics and corporate social responsibility gained momentum, particularly among the human rights activists, intellectuals and academicians leading to a new movement for better corporate governance. And serious discussions on *Corporate Governance and Corporate Social Responsibility (CSR)* began. Today, Corporate Social Responsibility or Business Ethics is not confined to the big corporations only but is equally applicable to all forms of Business and Professions- big or small.

'Business ethics has been a contested terrain'. There have been economists and *business gurus* who claim that ethics is irrelevant to the field of business. As for example, Milton Friedman of the Chicago school of economics and a Nobel Prize winner thinks that corporations are amoral and have only one responsibility, that is, to maximize profits. He also said that business cannot have social responsibilities. Peter Drucker, the great management guru said, *'there is neither a separate ethics of business nor is one needed'*. Peter Drucker, however, said on another occasion that *the ultimate responsibility of the directors of the companies is above all not to harm – primum non nocere*. The ideological position to exempt the corporate sector from of ethical obligations would defy understanding the social realities and commonsense. Ethics in business is necessary because, business can go unethical, and there are plenty of evidences of unethical business practices. Even Adam Smith, the great advocate of *laissez faire* had to say, *'People of the same trade seldom meet together, even for merriment and diversion, but the conversation ends in a conspiracy against the public, or in some contrivance to raise prices'*. It took a long time to understand that business does not operate in vacuum; all companies and firms operate in a social and natural environment and business is duty bound to be accountable to the society which sustains it.

Business ethics, also known as corporate ethics, is a form of applied ethics or corporate ethics that examines ethical and moral principles that arise in a business environment. It applies to all aspects of business conduct in all kinds of business operations and professions and is relevant to the conduct of individuals in business and business organizations as a whole. In the twenty-first century, business has to answer a wide array of questions covering all aspects of its operations, some of which are mentioned below:

(a) *General Ethics* concerns philosophy of business, ethics of governance (board room conspiracies), corporate social responsibility, political contributions, fiduciary responsibility, and shareholder vs. stakeholder concept, hostile take-overs, industrial espionage, and corporate manslaughter.

(b) *Ethics of Accounting and Financial* Information concerns: creative accounting, misleading financial analysis, insider trading, securities fraud, bribery, kickbacks, facilitation payments, executive compensations, breach of Auditors' code of conduct and conflict of interest in auditors' role as the watchdog.

(c) *Ethics of production* covers defective, addictive and inherently dangerous products and services (e.g. tobacco, alcohol, weapons, motor vehicles, chemical manufacturing, pollution, environmental ethics, carbon emissions trading, radiation and health, genetically modified food, animal rights, animal testing etc.

(d) *Ethics of Sales and Marketing* covers price fixing, price discrimination, price skimming, anti- competitive practices, spams (electronic), planned obsolescence, marketing in schools, viral marketing, black markets, grey markets, cyber crimes, media ethics and ethics of advertisements etc.

(e) *Ethics of Intellectual Property, Knowledge and Skills covers* patent, copyright and trademark infringements and misuse, bio-prospecting, bio-piracy, business intelligence, industrial espionage, employee raiding etc.

(f) *Ethics of Science and Technology.* The computer and the World Wide Web are two of the most significant inventions of the twentieth century. There are many ethical issues that arise from this technology. Similarly there are serious ethical questions on scientific, medical and biological experiments e.g. human genome project.

(g) *Ethics of International Business and Economic Systems* covers unfair trade, trade blocs, dumping, transfer pricing, child labour, bio prospecting, bio piracy in pharmaceutical industry, trading with oppressive regimes, economic sanctions, outsourcing of production and services to low-wage countries, globalization issues and cultural imperialism, global warming etc.

In an atmosphere of ever increasing public awareness and roles played by the civil societies in the twenty first century, the demand for greater ethical business processes and business operations is increasing. The *Bhopal gas tragedy* and the *Enron scandal*, triggered by bad business ethics, continue to remind the world about the need for stringent corporate ethics.

The world has been periodically rocked by corporate scams; in fact, as many as 67 major corporate scandals took place since 1980s till 2010. But, the first decade of the new millennium witnessed a series of corporate scandals unprecedented in human history in terms of their magnitude of scale and consequences. The global economic recession starting in 2008, a far greater recession than the Great Depression of 1930s, had been triggered by unethical and unscrupulous practices of some of the big corporates. Exotic financial instruments, unlimited greed and total disregard of fundamental business ethics on the part of a few individuals and corporate giants brought the entire world to the brink of disaster which all the governments of the world are still struggling to recover from.

Of the 37 major corporate scams which took place in the first decade, the following scandals created history in many ways and some of them were responsible for changing the course of corporate governance.

1. *Enron (2001),USA*

2. *WorldCom (2002), USA*

3. *Tyco International (2002),USA*

4. *Parmalat (2003), Italy*

5. *AIG (2004), USA*

6. *Lehman Brothers (2008),USA*

7. *Madoff (2008), USA*

8. *Washington Mutual,2008, USA*

9. *General Motors, 2009, USA*

10. *CIT Group, 2009, USA*

11. *Satyam Computers, 2009, India*

Some of the companies who filed for bankruptcies in the US courts of law had been the largest bankruptcies in US history of corporate giants who have assets worth several hundred billion dollars. The values of assets (as in 2009) involved in the bankruptcies of some of the companies are: Lehman Brothers - $ 686 billion, WorldCom - $126 billion, CIT Group - $72.1 billion, Enron Corp. - $77.9 billion, Chrysler -$39.9 billion, Texaco - $68.7 billion, Refco - $37.1 billion, Global crossing -36.5 billion, Delta Airlines -24.3 billion, Delfi Corporation - $ 23.3 billion, Conseco $74.2 billion, United Airlines - $30.5 billion, Washington Mutual - $332 billion, Pacific Gas and Betric co. - $36.6 billion and Financial Corp. of America - $62.3 billion.

The *Enron* scandal which led to the dissolution of the multi-national company and winding up of the leading financial company, *Arthur Andersen* prompted US Government to enact the famous *Sarbanes-Oxley Act* which sought to re-define corporate social responsibilities and the ground rules for corporate governance. Sarbanes-Oxley Act has been widely welcomed not only in the USA but also in all major industrial nations including India. The basic tenets of the Act have largely been adopted and framed into law by various countries of the world.

An analysis of the corporate scandals and scams of the first decade reveals certain interesting aspects of the phenomenon as indicated below:

(a) Most of the mega-scandals have taken place and continue to take place in the USA which has been the mother country for modern management theories and practices and the home of great Business Schools like Harvard and Wharton and of a large number management Gurus advancing the cause of business ethics.

(b) In all the scandals, very well-reputed Accounting and Auditing firms like Arthur Andersen, Price Waterhouse Coopers, Ernst & Young and KPMG were involved.

(c) In all the cases, the CEOs or the top management, especially the Finance Executives initiated and perpetrated the crimes.

(d) There was total lack of control on the part of the Regulatory Authorities who were either ineffective or chose to cast a blind eye on the wrong-doings of the companies.

(e) Personal ambitions, extreme greed and exotic financial instruments or creative accounting were responsible for the disasters.

(f) There was a definite collusion between the top management and the statutory auditors.

(g) Basic norms of business ethics were thrown overboard by the management. Even the basic framework given by Sarbanes-Oxley Act for corporate governance was grossly violated in almost all cases.

While a number of corrective measures have been taken by a number of countries like the constitution of Audit Committee of the Board, appointment of independent Directors on the Board, ensuring independence of Auditors, removing conflict of interests in auditing functions and financial functions, greater disclosure of financial results and greater oversight by the regulatory bodies, they are not enough to eliminate corporate scams and unethical practices of the corporate world. The world still wakes up to see new corporate scandals taking place mostly in the most developed countries which also have pioneered to bring greater transparency in the corporate world.

A number of other serious and relevant issues in corporate governance remain to be addressed. One of them has been the *management – ownership relationship.* The management-ownership relationship needs a review by which it is to be ensured that the ability for independent professional functioning of the Board of Directors is not jeopardized by the management structure. Another question which needs to be considered is the appointment of qualified Auditors on rotational basis and fixing their remuneration by an independent authority. Similarly, the question of inculcating ethical values among the Board members to put a stop to Board Room conspiracies which are still very much evident needs to be addressed. No doubt, there has been considerable progress in application of business ethics; however, it is a long way before the corporates show to the world greater transparency and a higher standard of ethics in corporate functioning.

Ethics of Public Administration and the raging debate on governance issues assume great importance in the context that the common man is adversely affected, at every step, on daily basis by the acts of commission and omission by the public administrators, much more than by the activities of the corporates. It is ironical that the State which is responsible for the legislations, for the implementation of the laws, for the implementation of the welfare programmes, for the delivery systems and for the protection of all citizens becomes the biggest tormentor of the common man and the common citizens become the helpless victims of corruption, mal-administration and discrimination. The law-makers become the law breakers, the governments grossly misuse their powers for personal benefits and the public servants become the masters. Greed, corruption and inefficiency creep into all levels of administration and a dangerous *vicious circle of police-politician-bureaucrat-businessman-criminal nexus* is formed to stifle democracy.

It is also ironic that the government which is the most organized sector where all decisions and actions are guided by the acts, rules and regulations and where the administrators are bound by strict rules of conduct, violates the ethics of governance at will taking us to the old adage, *all power corrupts and absolute power corrupts absolutely.* It is rather surprising that in spite of the existence of anti-corruption institutions, strict rules and regulations and training, a large number of highly enlightened and experienced bureaucrats succumb to greed, corruption and opportunism. Does it indicate that there has been total breakdown of the social and moral values which distinguish between the right and the wrong? Or does it mean that the legal protection of the civil service and the general lack of prosecution give them a sense of immunity from wrong- doing?

Ethics in Governance covers a vast area especially for a country like India where government functions at four levels – the central level, the state level, the local self-government level and the public undertakings level – where millions of *public servants* are involved. To establish uniform ethical standards of governance for the politicians, bureaucrats and the service providers at all the levels is an uphill task and may remain a dream only. But, establishment of proper systems of administration and a system of quick and exemplary punishment will certainly enhance the standards of governance.

Corruption has been the most significant and all-pervading manifestation of the failure of ethics in governance. The word corruption comes from the Latin word *corruptus* which means to break or destroy; that is why corruption is considered destructive. India has always been considered as one of the corrupt countries of the world. According to *Transparency International,* (2010), India ranks 87 with a *Corruption Perception Index* (CPI) of 3.3 as compared to China's 3.5 (rank 78) and Denmark, New Zealand and Singapore's 9.3 (rank 1 i.e. least corrupt). According to the *Ease of Doing*

Business Index (2010*),* another indicator of corruption, India ranks 133 indicating poor governance. In *Human Development Index* (HDI, 2010*),* yet another indicator of mal- administration, India ranks 134, almost at the bottom level.

Ethics in governance and possible measures to contain corruption can be grouped into five broad segments:

- *Ethics of the Law-makers and Legislators*
- *Ethics of the Ministers and Administrators*
- *Ethics of the Bureaucracy and the Civil Services*
- *Ethics of the Judiciary*
- *Ethics of the Public and the Private Sector.*

The 4rth Report of *the Second Administrative Reforms Commission* (ARC) of the Government of India on *Ethics in Governance* (2007) has made an in-depth study into the questions of corruption and ethics in governance in India. This report is not only a seminal scholastic treatise (perhaps the best available treatment of the subject in India), but also more revolutionary than what the Civil Societies are demanding. Its wide-ranging recommendations, if implemented, can comprehensively tackle the problem of corruption and usher in an era of high ethical standard in governance. The Report calls for a comprehensive reform in the political process, the electoral system, the judicial process and the bureaucracy. It has prescribed a code of conduct for the council of ministers, social audit, and protection of whistle-blowers and ethics of coalition government. It has also recommended establishment of a very strong *Lok Pal* for the Centre strong *Lok Ayukts* for all the States. It is surprising that no action has been taken or initiated on any of the major recommendations of the Commission contained in the 4rth Report. It appears these recommendations had escaped the notice of the government or they were found too radical for the present policy makers. Had the government accepted and implemented the 4rth Report of the Second ARC, there would been no agitational movement by Anna Hazare and other civil societies and the country would have got an effective Lokpal long ago.

In *'Ethics in Governance'*, the ARC made forty eight major recommendations for the establishment of enforceable ethics for political funding, the conduct of Parliamentarians and the Legislators of the State Assemblies, the Prime Minister, the Ministers, Bureaucrats, the Judges of the Supreme Courts and the High Courts, for the reform of the entire Electoral System, the Judicial System and the Administrative System and also for the creation of the *Lokpal* and the protection of the *Whistleblowers*. But, the government of the day which appointed the Administrative Reforms Commission having their own tall leader Veerappa Moily as its Chairman did not have any intention to implement any of the recommendations and scuttled them one by one through a bureaucratic process of getting them examined by a Committee of Secretaries. Look at the irony: recommendations of a high level Commission get rejected by a lower level committee of bureaucrats.

The Commission recognized that the bribe taker and the bribe giver are equally responsible and immoral and therefore, deserve equal punishment. It also recognized for the first time the role of the general public, the civil society and the private sector in establishing probity in public life. It is the private sector which has the resources to influence policies and the political process and receive favours by offering bribes in cash or in kind. It will be seen that the ARC has not left any important area of public life uncovered and the recommendations they have made are visionary having far-reaching consequences. The government, by ignoring the recommendations of the Commission it constituted, lost a golden opportunity in projecting itself as a well-intentioned and an ethical government.

Traditionally, especially in India, ethics is linked to individual morality and the social value-system handed down by religious and parental teachings. Swami Vivekananda, like Socrates, equated ethics with 'knowledge': *"We know that as knowledge comes, person grows, morality is evolved, and an idea of non-separateness begins. Whether men understand it or not, they are impelled by that power behind to become unselfish. That is the foundation of morality. It is the quintessence of all ethics, preached in any language, or any religion, or by any prophet in the world."* Mahatma Gandhi had a different view and equated ethics with virtue and absence of sins in society. Gandhi's perceptions of seven sins which he urged people to conquer were:

1. *Politics without principles*

2. *Wealth without work*

3. *Leisure without conscience.*

4. *Knowledge without character*

5. *Commerce without morality*

6. *Science without humanity*

7. *Worship without sacrifice.*

    (Young India, 1925)

Corruption has become a global phenomenon and poses the most difficult challenge to development and good governance. With rapid erosion and breakdown of the social value-system and individual moral values, this monster cannot be left to the individuals and the civil society to tackle. It has, therefore, been obligatory for the democratic governments to restore ethics with enforceable legislations. To say that *'ethics begins where law ends'* is not enough, particularly in a situation of fast-deteriorating standard in public life; it is necessary to convert ethics into enforceable law to regulate conduct of all actors who are responsible for governance. *The General Assembly in its Resolution 58/4 of 31ˢᵗ October, 2003* adopted the *United Nations Convention against Corruption*. Almost all the democratic governments in the developed world including the United States and the United Kingdom have enacted enforceable laws to remove corruption from public life and establish ethical governance system, an objective which has substantially been achieved in the European and American democracies. In India too, the largest democracy in the world, enforceable legislations like the *Lok Pal, Lok Ayukts, Citizens' Charter* and *Ombudsmen* would be necessary to establish ethics in governance and contain, if not kill the *monster of Corruption.*

VII

Why Didn't You Belong to us?

When my turn came for being posted as Additional Secretary in the Central Secretariat, the Government dragged its feet on a silly unwritten rule (which is always denied officially) that the Central Service Officers irrespective of their credentials and merits will be considered for promotion only after the IAS officers 2 years junior to them are accommodated in the Central Ministries. The idea was to indirectly eliminate non-IAS officers to compete for the Secretary's post in future. All right minded people in the Central Government thought it was unfair and was against creating a level- playing field for the bureaucrats but the biggest obstacle had been the Cadre System which tended to create invisible trade unions of their own. The IAS 'trade union' considered as the most powerful in the Central and State bureaucracies did not allow any intrusion into their rights and privileges; on the other hand, they would snatch away all the areas which can wield power. As for example, the post of Financial Advisors was created in the central ministries with a view to decentralize the powers of the Finance Ministry and these posts were to be manned by the officers of the Financial Services. When it was realized that these were growing to be rather powerful posts occupying a position next to the Secretary, almost all the posts were grabbed by the IAS cadre. The post of FA, if occupied by an IAS officer, was invariably upgraded to that of Additional Secretary when their turn for promotion arrived. This exactly happened in the Civil Aviation Ministry. When my turn for promotion to AS grade came, I was told in unequivocal terms that there was no proposal to upgrade the existing post of JS&FA to the level of Additional Secretary. But, within days of my shifting to the Ministry of Personnel, the same post was upgraded and an IAS officer many years junior to me was posted as Additional Secretary & Financial Adviser, Ministry of Civil Aviation.

In the Ministry of Personnel, I was posted to a 'graveyard post' known as Additional Secretary (Pension) which was not acceptable to any IAS officer. In addition to matters of pension, the post involved miscellaneous functions like Reorganization of States, Cadre Review of Central Services, and Cadre control of the Central Secretariat Service etc. which could not be allotted to other functionaries of the ministry. Additional Secretary (Pension) was also designated as the ex-officio Chairman of *Kendriya Bhandar*, the biggest Central Government Consumer Cooperative Society. I was also extremely reluctant to join the post but I was clearly told 'to accept it or leave it'.

VII

Creation of New States - Uttarakhand, Jharkhand and Chhattisgarh

One of the few things which gave some satisfaction in an otherwise drab situation had been the creation of the three new states of Uttarakhand, Jharkhand and Chhattisgarh, with which my department was very closely associated. Immediately after coming to power, the NDA government announced the creation of the three new states curving out of Uttar Pradesh, Bihar and Madhya Pradesh as part of implementation of their election manifesto. While the Congress Party expressed considerable scepticism about creating new states and termed it politically motivated, the majority of Indians thought the move was a positive one. In the case of Uttarakhand, there had been a *de facto* recognition for the State for a long time since the UP Secretariat had created a mini-Secretariat for Uttarakhand in Lucknow with a separate civil service for administering the hilly districts of UP. In the case of Jharkhand and Chhattisgarh, the aspirations of the vast majority of the tribal people could no longer be ignored. Therefore, there was practically no opposition to the proposals of creating three new States for the hilly and tribal peoples.

The task of the Ministry of Personnel, though limited to separation and placement of personnel belonging to the civil services, the Judiciary and the Legislative Assemblies, had been the most arduous task because of the inherent human problems, ego problems of the authorities, political pressures and the pulls and pressures brought in by the civil servants themselves.

A number of high-power committees were constituted by the Ministry to frame the principles of allocation and advice on the modalities for smooth transition of administration. One committee was formed at the central level to prepare the panels of officers belonging to the All-India Services (IAS and IPS); allocation of officers of the third All-India Service viz the Indian Forest Service was left to the Ministry of Environment and Forests which had been the cadre controlling authority. Three high power committees headed by retired officers of the status of Chief Secretary were constituted at the state level at Lucknow, Patna and Bhopal to prepare the lists of officers belonging to the State Services for their permanent allocation to the new States. Since these were inter-state issues, the final orders allocating the entire civil service between the states had to be issued by the Central Government. One of my Divisions in the Ministry was exclusively entrusted with the task of issuing final orders involving thousands of employees on the basis of recommendations made by the state-level committees. The state-level committees was entrusted with another quasi-judicial task, that of listening to the grievances of employees and their associations and adjudicating on in individual petitions and representations against allocation.

The task of the central committee was easier in that it had to deal with a small number and had only to determine the principles and criteria for allocation of the IAS and IPS officers to the newly created states and based on these criteria, the All- India Services Division of the Department of Personnel would issue the necessary orders. In the case of the state level committees, they had to work overtime. They had to deal with thousands of employees asking for their options, determine the basic principles of allocation, prepare separate lists for separate cadres including civil servants, teachers, doctors, lawyers, and engineers and also decide on the individual representations and petitions. The state level committees did a commendable job and accomplished an uphill task within a record time of three months. Without the deft and efficient handling of these committees, we could not have issued thousands of orders for the deployment of the employees, a condition which was essential for the functioning of the new states from the appointed dates.

While creation of Uttarakhand (initially Uttaranchal) and Jharkhand had been a rather painless affair, birth of Chhattisgarh had to undergo considerable labour pain. In the case of Uttarakhand, a separate secretariat of Uttarakhand had been functioning for a long time within the UP Secretariat at Lucknow. Therefore, it was a question of shifting the Uttarakhand Secretariat from Lucknow to Dehradun, the new capital of Uttarakhand. The division of the government cadres posed no problem as the senior and junior officers were allocated on 'as is where is' basis with a few exceptions. Moreover, enough volunteers were available who would be willing to serve the new state.

In the case of Bihar-Jharkhand, a peculiar situation arose. The number of volunteers especially among the senior cadres willing to serve the cash-rich and mineral-rich Jharkhand far outnumbered the posts created for the new state. This made the task of the stat-level committee easier. The committee could allocate either following the principle of seniority among the volunteers or the principle of pro-rata ratio distribution according to the relative size of the two states. The Bihar Committee had an unusual task of dealing with representations as to why their option for going over to the new state had not been accepted. However, in the end, the transfer of a few thousand employees was smoothly carried out.

The state level committee at Bhopal had a very difficult task to complete because very few officers from the various state cadres were willing to serve the new state of Chhattisgarh on permanent basis and therefore, did not volunteer for the new state. No set of principles could really work for MP- Chhattisgarh case. Therefore, the committee had to adopt a flexible approach to solve the problem. The local cadres who were not transferable outside their own districts falling within the jurisdiction of Chhattisgarh were automatically absorbed in the new state. Problems arose with the vast number of Group 'A' state service officers belonging to various disciplines like medical, engineering, education, finance etc. who were unwilling to go over to the newly created state. A compromise formula was devised under which all the unwilling officers selected on the basis of a fair policy of distribution would be initially sent on deputation basis and they would exercise within one year their final option for absorption in the new state or return to their old state. Special problems arose in regard to the officers belonging to the High Court at Jabalpur and the Vidhan Sabha. The Chief Justice of Madhya Pradesh High Court and the Speaker of Madhya Pradesh Assembly did not want their independence to be compromised in any manner and refused to accept the allocations made by the state level committee. They wanted the matter to be left to the discretion of the Chief Justice and the Speaker of the Vidhan Sabha to determine the fate of their respective officers.

My officers had to work on war-footing during this period and they had to sit late in the evening to process the recommendations received from the state level committees. Lists of officers were being received through fax messages on daily basis and as soon as they were approved, they were converted into office orders of the Government of India to be immediately sent to the respective state capitals. Fortunately, this process could be completed within the stipulated time well before the new states could start work in full swing. The two Directors who worked day and night to issue orders allocating the government servants to the three newly created states helping them to start functioning by the target date did not receive a word of praise from the higher echelons of the ministry. In fact, the Personnel Ministry headed by the Prime Minister was so impersonal that except me, the senior officers and the ministers did not even know their names.

IX

Thorn in the Hat

Additional Secretary (Pension) had many hats to wear; one of them had been *Kendriya Bhandar,* the biggest central consumer cooperative society which was managed by the Department of Personnel and the Additional Secretary (P) had been made the ex-officio Chairman. This had been an honorary job with no extra pecuniary or non-pecuniary benefits to the Chairman except transportation and a telephone. On the other hand, he had to work on holidays to enable him to concentrate on the pending cases and problems concerning *Kendriya Bhandar.* As far as I was concerned, I was fortunate to have as General manager, Mr. Sudarshan Synghal, an extremely able, sincere and honest IAS officer of the Madhya Pradesh Cadre, who did PhD in Economics from a US university but could not a good placement in the ministries of the Central Government because he lacked the essential connections with the political bosses. His family compulsions and commitments forced him to accept an innocuous post like that of General Manager, Kendriya Bhandar. However, this had been Kendriya Bhandar's gain and I could, without second thoughts, leave most of the decisions to him. He made Kendriya Bhandar a profitable organization with a turnover of more than

Rs.300 crore and handsome profits. Every year, we could hand over a respectable dividend cheque to the Minister of Personnel, who felt very happy to see that the cooperative society was making good profits.

But, my continuation as Chairman was made more and more uncomfortable by a host of MPs, disgruntled suppliers and a few corrupt employees who found me an obstacle to their way of functioning. Some of the employees were in collusion with some of the suppliers and some of the suppliers were in collusion with some of the MPs. There was a clear nexus between the suppliers and the politicians who instead of trying to improve the system were out to wreak the system by standing for the wrong people for personal gains. Kendriya Bhandar had been a thorn in my flesh during my entire tenure. Howsoever you wanted to get rid of it, it was not possible because the government made it a part of the Ministry of personnel and it was a part of normal duties of Additional Secretary (Pension). Ultimately, Kendriya Bhandar was freed from the control of the Ministry of Personnel and converted into an independent Cooperative Society with an elected Chairman but that was much after I demitted office. There was a starred Parliament Question asking about the rationale of Kendriya Bhandar being managed by the Ministry of Personnel and of the orders issued by the Ministry requiring all the Central Government Departments to buy stationary items and other office equipment from

Kendriya Bhandar only. Mr. Atal Behari Vajpayee, the Prime Minister had to answer the question in Parliament since he had also been the Minister in charge of the Ministry of Personnel. Mr. Vajpayee, being an astute, experienced and visionary politician decided, without second thoughts, that the government did not have any business to run a cooperative society and that it should not force the Departments to buy their requirements only from Kendriya Bhandar. Being in a monopolistic position and not having any competition, prices charged by Kendriya Bhandar had always been higher than the market price leading to loss of millions of rupees to the government. In the internal briefing meeting, Mr. Vajpayee asked us how soon the ministry would be able to reconstitute Kendriya Bhandar in accordance with the Central Cooperative Act and free the Society from the control of the ministry. We promised that it would be done within 6 months, a promise which the Ministry could not fulfil. It was finally done after almost 3 years, long after I left the ministry.

Chapter Five

A Peep Into Cag's Citadel

I

Return to the Roots

It was like the return of the prodigal son. Totally humiliated, frustrated and exhausted, I decided to come back to my parent department i.e. CAG's organization for the rest of my service career in the Central Government. Humiliated, because central secretariat is a ruthless place where everybody joins the rat-race to outdo others and pursue his selfish interests. Unless you dance to the tunes of the political bosses' whims and fancies and compromise your independence and judgement with their 'wishes', you will run the risk of being isolated and persecuted. A number of ministers whom I was not obliging and did not align with stopped calling me for any discussion and consultation and tried to spoil my confidential reports. The Secretaries also develop cold feet and you have to fend for yourself. It is sheer relationship of mutual benefit and *quid pro quo* between the ministers and the senior officers - you do my job and I do your job. I felt frustrated to work in such a situation of well-concealed agenda. I often felt it was below human dignity to work under such hypocrite ministers and spineless secretaries. The central Secretariat was no place for the honest and straight-forward officers. That is why it was not a surprise that the officer who topped the Civil Services Examination in our batch (Abhas Chatterjee) was never posted to the Central Secretariat and in his own home State, he was always harassed and humiliated with insignificant jobs. Ultimately, politics and humiliations led to his resignation from the Service and untimely death after resignation. Shortly after resignation, Abhas visited Jaipur to study the working of some of the NGOs as he wanted to devote the rest of his life to social service in his home state Bihar. Since I was working at Jaipur at that time, I chanced to meet him. We spent a whole evening chatting on the lawns of my official residence reminiscing old memories and sharing our own experiences. He recounted how he had to resist the pressures of the politicians and was shifted from one insignificant post to another and even then, there was no respite to harassment. When he was elevated as Transport Commissioner, he had to refuse the promotion because, according to him, there would definitely be greater demands on him to collect funds for the minister and the political party, which he would have refused to do. The higher you go up, the greater is the pressure to be enmeshed in the web of corruption. He was left with no alternative but to tender his resignation from the Service. Even after resignation, he could get no peace because of the vindictiveness of the State government. The State government was so vindictive and ruthless that they interpreted all the rules to deny him his legitimate pension. It is with the intervention of the central government that he could get the pensionary benefits due to him. He genuinely wanted to serve the people of Bihar but his honesty and uprightness antagonised the entire political spectrum and he resigned to his fate as a totally frustrated and broken man. "I think I have wasted my life" were his parting words full with pathos; we never met thereafter. A brilliant student who never stood second, a product of Delhi School of Economics, Abhas could have been an excellent successful Professor but destiny took him to the civil service where he was a total misfit. He was a die-hard non-conformist and I was a poor runner compared to him. He lost his job first, and then he lost his only son who died while trying to save another boy of his school being washed away by a swelling river and finally lost his own life while serving tribal people in remote rural areas of Chhattisgargh. The story of Abhas Chatterjee is one of the saddest stories of Indian civil service, a story of a genius destroyed by the politicians and a thoroughly corrupt system.

As for myself, extreme frustration awaited me in the Ministry of Personnel where I was working as Additional Secretary. I had forgone promotion in the CAG's Office with the expectation that in the normal course, the Additional Secretaries would find their place in the Secretary's Panel and that I would retire as a Secretary to Government of India, an expectation which could not be termed unreasonable. But I got a shock of my life when I got the news that I was not included in the Panel for Secretaries. Nothing remains secret in government. I was told that Brajesh Misra, Principal Secretary to the Prime Minister and Chairman of the Selection Committee asked the Personnel Secretary why his own Additional Secretary should not be included in the Panel. The Personnel Secretary's reply had been that under no circumstances, I should be empanelled and be made a Secretary. In other words, the Personnel Secretary was personally responsible for blocking my career in the Central Secretariat.

I was a fool and too naive not to realise this earlier. His personal dislike and prejudice had been evident from the beginning in all his dealings with me. He never looked happy with anything I did and did not behave 'normally' giving normal respect due to me because of my independent and straight-forward functioning. He was such an egotist that he could not tolerate any other officer getting any credit which was his monopoly. He expected his consent should be taken for each and every decision however minor they might be and even if they came under the delegated powers of the officers. I never went to him for decisions which came within my powers delegated to me.

It was my fault that I underestimated his prejudice against me. He was basically biased in favour of IAS officers and against other Service officers who tried to make their mark in the Central Secretariat. Incidentally, many officers belonging to the Central Services had outshone their counterparts belonging to IAS, a fact which the Personnel Secretary never wanted to acknowledge. I must admit I was forewarned by a Joint Secretary of the same ministry belonging to the Postal Service, who asked me in no uncertain terms that I should repatriate to the CAG's Organization because he was privy to the discussions which took place between the Personnel Secretary and two IAS officers both belonging to the UP Cadre (to which the Personnel Secretary also belonged) who spewed venom against me and wanted that I should be 'fixed.' These two officers (current Secretary, Civil Aviation and the other a former Joint Secretary of the same ministry) used to visit the Personnel Secretary's office in order to salvage the reputation of the Joint Secretary who had been charged by the CBI for grave misconduct and corruption. I was held squarely responsible for the CBI charges because the CBI took cues from the decisions taken in the Air-India Board of which I was a Government Director.

Every time they met the Secretary my name cropped up hurling abuses and the obvious need to 'fix' me would be stressed. It was difficult to believe but it was true. But the breaking point came later when the Telecom Secretary (a batch-mate of mine) praised me in a meeting with the Cabinet Secretary for giving an excellent pension scheme for the employees of the newly constituted BSNL. The scheme was acceptable to the Telecom Department which proposed to hand over their residual (they earlier created MTNL and VSNL) telecom service operations to a Public Sector Company named Bharat Sanchar Nigam (BSNL), a giant service provider in the public sector for the whole country except two cities, Mumbai and Delhi which would be under MTNL. The separation of a vast number of personnel was becoming difficult and was strongly resisted by the highly unionised employees of the telecom department who would not move an inch without being assured of an equivalent pension scheme at par with the Central Pension Scheme. I was inducted in an inter-ministerial committee constituted by the Telecom Department, where I gave the Pension plan as a member of the committee. The Ministerial Committee constituted for this purpose accepted the scheme and the trade unions were also persuaded to accept it. The Personnel Secretary had nothing to do with this innovative effort. After the final meeting with the Cabinet secretary (where I was also present) giving the final seal to the scheme was over, I heard a commotion at the departure gate of Rashtrapati Bhawan where the Personnel Secretary was shouting at the top his voice as to why did the Telecom secretary give the credit for the scheme to me and not to the Personnel secretary (who had the 'copy-right' of the officers of the Personnel Ministry). The Telecom Secretary tried to argue in vain that being one his officers, he thought he would be happy if he praised the good work done by me to the Cabinet Secretary. But the Personnel Secretary was wild with rage and started treating me almost as a traitor thereafter.

It is in this background that I wrote to the CAG for my immediate repatriation to my parent organization. Soon, orders were received to release me from the Central Secretariat 'prison'. I experienced a strange feeling of relief, peace and tranquillity. Perhaps, there was a sense of hurt and disgrace while handing over the charge in the ministry. My only regret was that a person who had honestly and sincerely worked as Under Secretary, Deputy Secretary, Joint Secretary and Additional Secretary in various ministries was not found worthy of working as Secretary just because he belonged to IAAS and not IAS and only because some corrupt ministers tried to spoil his CRs and did not give him 'outstanding' reports. I wrote a very strong letter to the Prime Minister's Office pointing out the system and criteria for selection of Secretaries in Government of India were seriously flawed. The basic criteria of successive 'outstanding' reports were fraught with dangerous consequences. First, getting outstanding reports at any cost had become the sole mantra of officers of the Secretariat, which involved compromising their positions and surrendering to the political whims. Secondly, the Selection Committee should apply its mind as to the credentials of the reporting officers and the ministers who had given outstanding reports. As for example for certain posts like that of the Financial Advisers who are accredited to more than one ministry, it was impossible to get the confidential reports completed on time because of involvement of at least two secretaries and two ministers and even if that was done, it was an impossibility to secure outstanding reports because of the nature of the job. I further pointed out that if I received 'outstanding' reports from Mr. 'M' or Mr. 'N' who were notorious for their muscle power, money power and political clout, the Selection committee should have come to the conclusion that something was wrong with me and if I received adverse reports from these gentlemen, the Committee should have pondered that perhaps, I had done an honest job. That was the reason why the entire Central Secretariat was full of 'compromised' officers who immensely benefited for following the path of least resistance. Honesty never paid and honest officers had no protection. The PMO agreed with my viewpoint and circulated my letter to the higher authorities. It created a flutter but ended in smoke because nothing happened to make any dent in the system.

Coming back to my own organization gave me a feeling of the boy lost in a crowded *mela* ultimately finding and embracing his own parents. I could breathe a gush of fresh air in a pristine atmosphere away from the highly polluted culture with stifled freedom. There would be no minister to breath down your neck, no interference in your area of work and no boss to please. Traditionally, the CAG never interferes in the technical functions of the senior officers and never demands any adulation and any deviation from the long tradition was an exception. Officers are given long ropes. It is expected that the Audit Reports which are to be presented in Parliament/Legislature should be foolproof, well-documented, investigative and of highest standard. Since CAG has special relationship (as *friend, guide and philosopher*) with the Public Accounts Committees of the Parliament and of the State Legislatures, senior officers are expected to be extremely careful in dealing with the Parliamentary Committees because it is only from these committees that the CAG receives unflinching support and strength in an otherwise hostile world.

II

CAG - the Most Coveted Post, but Who Fits the Shoes?

The top bureaucrats soon realised that the post of CAG is the most coveted post in the entire country - the highest post which any bureaucrat can ever dream to reach. So a rat race started in late 1970s to grab this post by any means. It is forgotten that the CAG's organization is a specialised organisation and the Indian Audit & Accounts Service (IAAS) which constitutes the managerial level of the organisation is a specialised and technical Service. The IAAS which is one of the oldest constituted Services, if not the oldest, was created alongside the ICS and owes its origin to the hallowed Office of the Accountant General, Bengal (AG Bengal) which had financial jurisdiction over the whole of British India under the East India Company. In 1780s, AG, Bengal, obviously manned by a British Officer, had been the highest paid officer of the East India Company with a remuneration of one lakh rupees per year, an unbelievably high salary those days. After the British Crown took over the East India Company's Administration and replaced it by the His Majesty's Government in 1860, a number of administrative, financial and technical services were constituted. Of these, the ICS and IA&AS became two formidable services. Power, prestige, high salary and eliticism attracted a large number of talents from all walks of life. These services developed great expertise, great reputation and great efficiency inviting the nomenclatures like 'steel- frame' and 'incorruptible'. The ICS was abolished after Independence but the IAAS has had the unbroken tradition and continuity of over 150 years. It is difficult to believe that even the great C.V. Raman, the Nobel Laureate Physicist had been a member of the IA&AS. When he was working in one of the AG offices in Calcutta, Sir Ashutosh Mukherjee spotted him and appointed him as a faculty in Calcutta University where in an ill-equipped dark room, with obsolete instruments, he discovered his Nobel Prize winning "Raman Effect". The ethos and traditions of the department were no less glorious than those of the ICS.

That had been the reason why after Independence and launching the world's best written Constitution, the Constitution Makers made the CAG a Constitutional Authority. While doing this, the main architect of the Indian Constitution commented that the CAG was *perhaps the most important officer of the Constitution*. The CAG had invariably been appointed from among the IAAS officers. Pandit Nehru who had been a great democrat and a great institution builder never allowed any thought of manipulating appointment to this august office either by outsiders or by top bureaucrats.

Therefore, till Nehru had been the Prime Minister, all the three CAGs appointed during his time, were from the IAAS and Nehru did not make any mistake in selecting people. Narahari Rao, A.K.Chanda and A.K.Roy were stalwarts in their own rights and these tall officers took the CAG's Organisation to newer heights. While Nehru was personally distressed by CAG's damaging reports against Krishna Menon (Nehru's most favourite personal friend and a fellow traveller) who was found involved in the Jeep scandal and the Gun Powder scandal, he never said anything against the CAG or the PAC; the democrat in him told him that CAG was only doing his duty. His respect for CAG never diminished even after his government was badly hit by CAG's functions. Nehru set a healthy precedent and tradition that one Constitutional functionary, be it the Parliament or the Judiciary or the CAG shall not criticise the other Constitutional Authorities. During Nehru's time, CAG was never commented upon and not even mentioned in Parliament nor was he summoned by any Parliamentary Committee. Of course, the CAG has always been intimately associated for technical help and guidance with the most powerful committees of Parliament – the Public Accounts Committee (PAC) and the Committee on Public Undertakings (COPU). Nehru's tradition continued for a pretty long time through Indira Gandhi, Rajiv Gandhi, Narasimha Rao and Atal Behari Vajpayee etc. till 2011. This beautiful unwritten convention set by Pandit Nehru was thrown to the winds in 2012 when cornered by a number of damning Audit Reports on a number of scams, Prime Minister Manmohan Singh, his ministers and a large number of parliamentarians started a crusade against the CAG and his powers.

Instead of complimenting the CAG for producing historic reports revealing mega corruption scandals which caused losses to the nation to the tune of billions of rupees, the ruling political class rose against a constitutional authority in unprecedented virulence because they had feet of clay. This was a clear indication of subversion of democracy and of the Constitutional traditions.

An incident which took place between Nehru and Narahari Rao reveals the true character of this great democrat who used to call himself (which he genuinely believed in) *the first servant of the nation.* Narahari Rao had an appointment with Nehru and he reached Nehru's office on time but the Prime Minister was still busy in an urgent meeting. Narahari Rao who waited for five minutes came back to his office leaving a small note 'I think the CAG of India cannot be kept waiting for more than five minutes'. When the meeting was over and Nehru saw the note, he immediately rang up Narahari Rao and apologized for the incident and fixed another time for the meeting and promised to be free to receive him. This was Nehru and this was the quality of great humble democrat. I think except Lal

Bahadur Shastri, his worthy successor, there has been no Prime Minister in India who could be so humble. Of course Lal Bahadur is simply incomparable. There is perhaps no instance in history of a Prime Minister insisting on spending a night with a farmer family in a remote village without electricity and sharing the same *dal roti* which the housewife made and sleeping on the same *charpai* which they slept on. This he did during his official visit to AMUL at Anand, Gujarat.

I have noticed that the dignity and effectiveness of the Constitutional Office of the CAG have been in direct proportion to the degree of democratization and Constitutionalism nurtured by the successive Prime Ministers. The high tradition of mutual trust and respect was broken for the first time by Indira Gandhi in 1972 when she squarely blamed the CAG for her defeat in the court case against her election and went to the extent of stripping the CAG of his powers to maintain the Accounts of the Central Government by bringing an amendment to Article 148 of the Constitution. The Allahabad High Court quashed her election to the Parliament for resorting to unfair means which was proved by the documents and vouchers produced by AG, UP, an officer of the CAG. S. Ranganathan, the then CAG was rather forced to demit his office in protest, the only case of a CAG resigning because of differences with the government.

While Pandit Nehru had been a great builder of institutions and painstakingly built one institution after another, his daughter, when faced with crisis situations, painstakingly destroyed many institutions to strengthen her own political standing. She invented the concept of "committed bureaucracy". She wanted everything committed to her policy – committed party, committed bureaucracy, and committed judiciary and also committed CAG. She knew very well that there should be only one commitment for all, that is, commitment to the Constitution of India. Slowly, the bureaucracy, the police, and a section of the judiciary started forgetting their basic commitment to the Constitution and the Law and started dancing to the political tunes. The only colour visible to them was the political colour.

The CAG did not bow his head and this had been the only institution which kept itself totally free from being polluted by the political colours. The division of the department was meant to weaken the organisation but the opposite happened– instead of getting weakened, the CAG's organisation and its audit functions strengthened and expanded in new areas and was imbibed by new ideas and new techniques. CAG's became a founder member of International Organisation of Supreme Audit institutions (INTOSAI) which came out with new Auditing Standards for all countries. The Indian CAG has played an important role in the international arena – as Auditors of the United Nations and Affiliated Institutions, as an active member of the Supreme Audit Institutions (SAI) and its various committees to improve auditing functions, as organiser of bilateral exchange of ideas, officers and seminars with major countries like China, USA, UK, Australia, Japan, Poland etc, as a trainer of senior officers of SAIs on regular basis and by creating a world-class international centre for computer based research in audit named International Centre for Information Systems and Audit (ICISA). Close interactions with the Auditor Generals of all the major nations, being on the Board of Auditors of the United Nations, being sole External Auditor of a number of UN Specialized Agencies like WHO and FAO, acceptance of international standards of auditing and adoption of modern computer-based techniques of auditing have provided the CAG of India a rock-like foundation which no political party and no hostile government can really shake.

The Achilles heel of the CAG's Organisation has been the process of selection and appointment to this august post. There is no well- established system of appointment of appropriate, eligible and experienced persons to this dignified Constitutional post. Everything about appointment of the CAG is shrouded in mystery. This has perhaps been the only high post for which rules of appointment has not been notified and unlike Judges of the Supreme Court with whom CAG has been equated, there is no Collegium, nor a high-level Committee with the leader of the opposition and the Speaker of Lok Sabha. Transparency has been a casualty.

III

'What Transparency? I Appoint Them!'

Excepting the first three CAGs - Narahari Rao (1948-1954), A.K.Chanda (1954-1960) and A.K.Roy (1960-1966) during the Nehru era when they almost selected themselves with no interference from the Prime Minister and other quarters (nobody had the courage to do so against Nehru's wishes), all the other CAGs appointed subsequently had been the personal choice of the Prime Minister. This was the only Constitutional dignitary whom the Prime Ministers could appoint arbitrarily without following any procedure. The Finance Ministry which is the nodal ministry for CAG does the initial processing based on certain arbitrary criteria (the informal norms are kept close to their chest) and prepares a panel of three persons found suitable for appointment as CAG. The Finance Minister finalises the panel and recommends three names in order of preference to the Prime Minister.

It is not known if the recommendations of the Finance Minister have ever been accepted; probably not. On many an occasion, the Finance Minister had recommended the senior- most Deputy CAG (a post equivalent to the Secretary to Government of India) and other officers who possess wide-ranging expertise in Public Finance and Public Auditing but the panel simply 'vanishes' when it reaches the Prime Minister's Office (PMO). By the time the panel reaches the PMO, the Prime Minister has already made up his mind about whom he should appoint as CAG, a person of his confidence who would not embarrass him and who would be an effective tool in taming the opposition leaders. He either chooses a name outside the panel or a name from the panel if it coincides with the name he has in mind. The Principal Secretary to the PM exercises considerable influence in the matter of selection of the CAG and does the basic groundwork appointing himself as the single-member search committee. On some occasions, it is reported, the Principal Secretary threw away the entire panel and put the name of PM's choice for appointment as CAG and sent the single name to the President for his final seal of approval. Personal equations of the prospective officers with the PMO and their accessibility to the Prime Minister also play a great role in the process of selection. On one occasion, when the whole world was busy discussing big names in the Government finding their names in the so-called panel, a dark horse believed to be too close to the PM's family was suddenly appointed as the CAG. Therefore, transparency has always been the casualty after Nehru-era. The argument given by the PMO has always been that there has been a procedure in place and the selection is made by the Prime Minister after careful consideration of all the prospective candidates for the post. A question may arise, why should it not go to the Appointment Committee of the Cabinet or a specially constituted Selection Panel consisting of the Speaker of the Lok Sabha and the Leader of the Opposition? One may argue in defence of the Prime Minister 'for God's sake, let there be at least one Constitutional dignitary on which the Prime minister should have exclusive right for appointment and let it be the CAG!'

But there has been an irony of fate in almost all cases of such appointments. The PM's most trusted or favourite nominee has always turned against the same government which appointed them by producing most embarrassing and devastating Audit Reports to the Parliament, not by design but by the compulsions of office. With one or two exceptions, all CAGs have tried to be true to their oath of office and maintain the dignity, impartiality, efficiency, sense of duty and justice befitting the Judge of the Supreme Court with whom he has been equated. No CAG has, because of his oath, tried to influence the traditions and expertise of the Indian Audit and Accounts Department which is more than 150 years old and stop the uninterrupted flow of Audit Reports (about 100 Reports a year) on the Central Government, the State Governments, Autonomous Institutions and the Public Sector undertakings, some of which had been responsible for toppling the governments or severely damaging the credibility of the Administrations.

Little is known about how the fourth CAG, S. Ranganathan, ICS (1966-1972) had been appointed and why an exception was made in not appointing an IAAS officer as CAG. There was already thinking at the higher level that the CAG should alternately be from the South and it is probably T.T. Krishnamachari who influenced the decision in his favour treating Ranganathan as a finance man. When a delegation of IAAS officers met Indira Gandhi on the issue, she assured that the CAG would henceforth be selected from among the IAAS officers, a promise which she had herself broken when she found it expedient to appoint T. N. Chaturvedi succeeding Ardhendu Bakshi. After Bakshi, the last IAAS CAG, there was a deluge and the IAS lobby grabbed this post which no politician, however powerful, could reverse the damage.

Ranganathan had been an honourable person. He could not take the insult heaped on him by Mrs. Gandhi who, without consulting him (which was mandatory under the Constitution) went on vindictively to amend the Constitution, bifurcate the CAG's Organisation and create a separate Central Civil Service called Indian Civil Accounts Service by taking away the accounting functions of the entire Central Government. Her vindictive actions followed the judgement of the

Allahabad High Court declaring her election to Parliament null and void mainly based on the vouchers produced by the Accountant General, Uttar Pradesh showing misuse of government funds during election campaign in her constituency. The action of the AG did not call for knee-jerk reaction because any accounting authority, be it under the CAG or under the Central Government was bound to produce the vouchers under the court orders. The perception of the ruling party might have been that with the CAG, the production of records could not be manipulated but had it been with the Central Government, the vouchers need not have been produced! So, Ranganathan demitted office prematurely, albeit a few months before his tenure was due to end. This was the only case in the history of the Indian Audit and Accounts Department that a serving CAG resigned from the Constitutional post (out of moral remorse because he could not prevent bifurcation of the Department), which he need not have done at all because the CAG could not be removed without an impeachment in Parliament.

The fifth CAG, Ardhendu Bakshi (1972-1978) had been appointed by Indira Gandhi because he vehemently supported her move to nationalise the major banks of India when he was Deputy Governor of the Reserve Bank of India. Indira Gandhi brought Ardhendu Bakshi to the Central Secretariat as the Secretary to the newly created Department of Banking following

'Bank Nationalisation' in 1968 and subsequently, appointed him as the CAG of India thus fulfilling her promise to appoint an IAAS officer as the CAG after Ranganathan.

Ardhendu Bakshi's tenure was marked by needless controversies about his style of functioning and personal idiosyncrasies, which overshadowed his achievements in improving the quality of Audit Reports. If A. K. Roy is remembered for the expansion of the Department, upliftment of the Audit Service making it very attractive and introduction of the concept of Revenue Audit, A. K. Bakshi would be remembered for his big leap in 'Value for Money Audit', 'Efficiency–cum–Performance Audit', 'Audit Reviews or Audit Appraisals of Major Projects and Schemes'. His Audit Reports on 'Command Area development Programmes' and 'Drought-Prone Areas Programme' which bore the stamp of his personal supervision and drafting had been seminal and pioneering works in the field of public auditing. The content and quality of Audit Reports received a quantum jump during his tenure, unsurpassed by any of the Auditor Generals. Here was an unusual Auditor General burning midnight oil glossing over every word and sentence of 100-odd draft Audit Reports every year giving new meaning to them. His commitment to take the CAG's Organisation to a new level of efficiency making it an effective instrument of public accountability with the active support of the

Public Accounts Committee earned him many enemies within the Establishment. People misunderstood him more easily than trying to understand his intentions. He was a socialist and extremely humanitarian in his approach. He believed that public expenditure should result in public good and if the government schemes do not bring public good, the schemes and the methods of administering the schemes deserve to be criticised and brought to the notice of the Parliament and the state legislatures. Therefore, all his Audit reviews focussed on whether the targeted beneficiaries have actually benefited from the schemes or whether the public funds have been unnecessarily frittered away. Any objective assessment of Ardhendu Bakshi would put him in the category of a great Auditor General.

After Ardhendu Bakshi there was an invasion by self-seeking bureaucrats trying to grab this lucrative post. 1978 had been a turning point in the history of the Audit and Accounts Department when an IAS officer Gian Prakash was appointed for the first time as CAG of India. Since then the IAS lobby did not let this Constitutional post slip out of their grip and thereafter, nobody except an IAS officer has been appointed as CAG. The IAS lobby has succeeded in reducing this august Constitutional post to a cadre post of the Indian Administrative Service and the political bosses, while they knew it was wrong, did not do enough to break the bureaucratic stranglehold, rather they meekly submitted to bureaucratic lobbying because it suited their political interests. When a new CAG was to be appointed in 2002, in the capacity of President of IAAS Officers Association, I had met Manmohan Singh, then Leader of the Opposition in Parliament and Pranab Mukherjee, then in the opposition during NDA regime, urging the need to revert back to the system of appointing a senior IAAS officer as CAG mainly because the post needed wide-ranging experience in Auditing and Accounting. In fact, when I met Pranab Mukherjee in his office, the first question he asked me was: 'Tell me, why the CAG should be appointed from outside the Department?' I was rather overwhelmed by his concern. He also disclosed an unknown fact that he had, in his early years, worked for some time as Auditor in the office of the Accountant General, West Bengal. Both of them assured that they would certainly take up the issue with the Prime Minister, Atal Behari Vajpayee. But in the end, they did nothing to change the system nor did they give any public statement on the issue.

The appointment of the sixth CAG, Gian Prakash (1978-1984) was queer. He superseded two ICS officers who were far more experienced, had vast experience in Finance and administration and had far greater credentials for holding the post. It is believed that Chaudhary Charan Singh, Deputy Prime Minister and Finance Minister in the Janata Government headed by Morarji Desai (which was on the point of collapse and Charan Singh was to be made the interim Prime Minister), was insistent that Gian Prakash, Defence Secretary be made the CAG. It was rumoured that Chaudhary Charan Singh wanted to favour Gian Prakash because of his personal relations with him. So, the candidature of H.N.Ray, ICS who had been the Finance Secretary or of M.M.Sen, ICS, the Secretary, and Defence Production was overthrown. Gian Prakash, during his entire tenure, could not understand, love or hate the Audit department and could not come up with any vision which the Department could remember.

The seventh CAG, T. N. Chaturvedi (1984-1990) was also appointed in queer circumstances. Chaturvedi had been the Home Secretary in Indira Gandhi's government but Mrs. Gandhi being an advocate of 'committed bureaucracy' wanted to replace him by an officer who would be more 'committed' to her and was looking for an opportunity to park him. An immediate opportunity arose in1984 when the post of CAG was to fall vacant. Mrs. Gandhi took the opportunity and posted Chaturvedi as the seventh CAG of India. No one knows if any credible procedure was followed in his case but, the fact remains that during her regime, nobody had the courage to question Mrs. Gandhi's decision. T. N. Chaturvedi did not hide his lack of experience in the complexities of Auditing and Accounting principles and practices. He promoted what he knew best, that is, training. He made a good contribution in starting training of all officers and staff from the grass-root level and established training institutions for intensive training in Auditing and Accounting in almost all States. At the national level he conceived an International Institute for imparting training and research for officers of the Supreme Audit Institutions and mainly for Afro-Asian and Oceania countries, an effort which had been immensely successful. He also upgraded the existing IAAS Training School, Shimla as National Academy of Audit and Accounts.

Another major contribution of T. N. Chaturvedi had been the initiative taken by him to get India elected to the UN Board of Auditors, a very powerful body of the United Nations Organization. The Board consists of three member nations represented by their Auditor Generals for a 4-year term for conducting audit and reporting on the activities of the UN organizations and their offices located in various parts of the world. This had been a big diplomatic move which required support of the Indian Government and a large number of foreign powers. The initiative bore fruit only after Chaturvedi demitted office.

T. N. Chaturvedi's tenure was marked by publication of a few significant Audit Reports like 'Bofors Scandal' 'Main Battle Tank' etc. It may be remembered that it is the Audit Report on the Bofors Gun Deal that created a storm and ultimately led to the fall of the Rajiv Gandhi Government. While a number of such explosive reports had been published in the past, it is the scandal associating the name of the Prime Minister that created the storm. In the same Audit Report volume, the report on the construction of the Main Battle tank for the Army had been a more explosive report but the report neither received any publicity nor was it discussed in the PAC or the parliament. T. N. Chaturvedi had been very media- friendly and he succeeded in bringing the Audit Reports in the domain of public debate.

The eighth CAG had been a retired IAS officer, C.G.Somiah (1990-1996) who was working as the Chief Vigilance Officer (CVC) at the time of his appointment (which perhaps added to his credentials to hold the post of CAG). Somiah said that P.V. Narasmha Rao called him and asked him to take over as the CAG as he was looking for an apolitical and honest officer for this Constitutional post. But what was forgotten that the CAG needed to be an expert in finance having wide experience in auditing and accounts.

Somiah started well. But after a by-pass surgery of his heart, which gave him a rude shock, he slowed down and lost interest in providing necessary momentum to the development of the Department; in fact, he was never tired of mentioning his dislike for the Department by quoting examples of unfair treatments he received from the Accountant General's office while working as a Secretary to the Government of Orissa. I noticed that he could never love the Audit Department. He immersed himself in globe-trotting visiting almost all the UN establishments, big or small, which came under the audit jurisdiction of the UN Board of Auditors. India got elected to the UN Board of Auditors for the first time during his tenure, for which T. N. Chaturvedi did all the spadework and lobbying. Somiah enjoyed the fruits of efforts made during Chaturvedi's time and bid his time with a small coterie of advisors from the South.

The ninth CAG, V.K.Shunglu (1996-2002), was handpicked by the Prime Minister superseding the panel of three names (in which the name of the senior most Deputy CAG also figured) processed and forwarded by the Finance Ministry. Notwithstanding his being a generalist IAS officer and not having specialist knowledge in Auditing and Accounting, Shunglu had been one of most dynamic CAGs the Department have had. He had been bold, straightforward, decisive, effective and forward looking and at the same time had been very respectful of the traditions of the department and its officers. Shunglu, a Kashmiri belonging to the Gujarat Cadre, had the outstanding capability of carrying with him the officers of the department, the bureaucracy, the government and the PAC. During his tenure, the Audit Reports both on the Indian governments and on the international institutions received wide acclamations and his efforts took the Audit Department to a new height. He personally supervised the designing and construction of the new imposing building for the Shimla Academy and the new complex for the International centre for Information Systems and Audit (ICISA) at NOIDA. He also made the blueprint for the new headquarters office building to be constructed later at New Delhi's Deen Dayal Upadhyay Marg. Shunglu's leadership and achievements made all the officers and staff proud again of the Audit Department.

The tenth CAG had been V. N. Kaul (2002-2008), another Kashmiri who had been a dark horse in the race for the CAG's post when bigger names were going the rounds just before Shunglu was due to demit office. Till the last moment, his name was never mentioned anywhere as a contender and a sudden announcement of Kaul's appointment as the next CAG surprised the entire bureaucratic circle as well the Audit Department and was received with mute scepticism. It was rumoured that Kaul who had been working as the Petroleum Secretary had undergone a heart surgery and was seeking a 'lighter job' like that of CAG and he got the job because of his close relationship with the Prime Minister's family. Kaul's tenure was marked by confusion about the Constitutional responsibilities the CAG was expected to perform and about the Mandate of the CAG. Even in public forums and national television programmes, Kaul could not and did not defend the CAG against the criticism of politicians and the government as regards performance audit. No questions were asked for the last 40 years about CAG's conducting performance audit of various schemes and projects started in a big way by A. Bakshi and continued by all CAGs till the Central Government was hit hard by the reports on 2-G scam, the Coal scam and the Commonwealth Games. Kaul forgot that Performance audit or value for money audit had already become a part of the normal audit of the CAGs all over the world including the UN Organizations and was mandated by the Auditing Standards (which was adopted by all member countries) of the International Organization of Supreme Audit Institutions (INTOSAI) of which India is an important member. Kaul's commitment to the Audit Department had been ambivalent and his public speeches and statements on CAG's powers aired in the media lowered the image of the CAG in public eye.

The eleventh CAG, Vinod Rai (2008-2013) had been an exception to the general mill of IAS turned CAGs and proved to be an exceptional CAG who faced unprecedented hostilities emanating from the Prime Minister, senior Ministers and Parliamentarians of the ruling party. He endured all humiliations with a smile including being summoned by a Parliamentary Committee (which never happened in history because CAG is a Constitutional Authority) without losing the dignity of the office. More like Shunglu, he galvanised the whole Audit Department to perform and produce a number of outstanding reports which rocked the Manmohan Singh Government. While he was selected by Manmohan Singh, his commitment to his Constitutional duties and to the Audit Organisation embarrassed the government to the maximum and did not hesitate to expose the government's endemic maladministration. Vinod Rai gave a new dimension to the audit reports focussing on corruption in public life and giving them a public face. He succeeded in making his reports instruments of public debate; otherwise, most of the reports would have gathered dust in the distant corners of PAC and of the government departments without being discussed or taking any action on them. He adopted the best practices and techniques in auditing and brought new enthusiasm in the CAG's Organisation.

IV

Of Professionalism and Conflict of Interest

While most the later CAGs had been Prime Minister's men, many of them did not remain so when they realised the nature of Constitutional responsibilities and the import of what B.R.Ambedkar expected of them to be the 'most important officer of the Constitution'. These CAGs rose above their previous Service affiliations and political loyalties and made their mark in their new *avatars*. But two questions which have been agitating the minds of intellectuals and the officers of the Audit Department have not been addressed by the Government for the last three decades. These are: (a) whether the CAG should not be a professional and proficient in his job which is of technical nature demanding specialist skill in public auditing and accounting and (b) whether there is an inherent conflict of interest in appointing a generalist IAS administrator who heads a number of departments in the Central as well as State governments? The Central Government have so far carefully skirted these questions and have been appointing generalist IAS officers without having a transparent procedure. This has probably done deliberately because they do not want a powerful CAG and have always wanted a yes man.

Ever since these issues were raised by H.D.Shourie in 'Common Cause', an organisation for Public Interest Litigations (PIL), attempts have been made to file a PIL case every time a new CAG is appointed. When the twelfth CAG (Shashi Kant Sharma) was appointed in May, 2013, a Public Litigation was filed with the Supreme Court which rejected it. A similar petition had been pending in Delhi High Court for a long time, was finally disposed of without any verdict.

The arguments are quite logical but the government of the day has to accept the logic and without the government's appreciation and acceptance of the logic, no progress in this matter is possible. In almost all democratic countries in the world, the Auditor General is appointed from the professionals specialising in Auditing and Financial Management because the work of the Auditor General is treated everywhere as a technical job. It is in India that the Government of India has deluded itself with the idea that a generalist can function better than a specialist and hold any post in the government. This has created a considerable credibility gap vis-à-vis Auditor Generals of the advanced countries. In the international forums, the Indian Auditor General, however stoic look he may take and however proud he may be of the expertise of his officers, he cannot command the same respect as is commanded by the technically sound Auditor Generals of advanced democracies like UK, USA, France, Germany, Japan and Israel. Therefore, it is ridiculous to argue and appoint a generalist as the CAG of India. In fact, it an irony and mockery perpetrated on a Constitutional post.

The second issue which has been the main issue, apart from the question of transparency, in the Public Interest Litigation is the conflict of interest. IAS officers work for the state as well as for the Central Government and at senior levels, they head a number of Departments in the State and at the Centre. They become an integral part of the political system and are responsible for policy making and implementation of various schemes and programmes. Here lies the problem. How could a CAG who had been responsible for the implementation of projects, schemes and programmes including acquisitions for the government effectively audit and report against themselves? As for example, a CAG who had worked as Defence Secretary is directly or at least morally responsible for various acts of omissions and commissions in multi- billion dollar contracts for purchase of military hardware. How can the same CAG criticise his own policies and decisions taken along with his political bosses and report against those decisions to the Parliament? Is it to be assumed that the Defence Secretary cannot be blamed for any of the scams frequently occurring in defence deals? This is absurd. Defence Audit has been one of most important and vital areas of CAG's Audit not only because of the magnitude of the deals but also because of their implications on the national security. Therefore, there is an obvious conflict of interest in appointing a CAG who had worked as Defence Secretary. Similar is the situation if any of the Secretaries to Government of India is appointed as the CAG.

This bitter truth does not dawn on the government. The government of the day irrespective of the party affiliation is too blind and arrogant to listen to the rational voices and deviate from their feudalistic patronage predilections.

V

CAG Goes Global

Ever since the Indian CAG was elected to the UN Board of Auditors in early 1990s, the CAG's organization started receiving international attention with increasing interest. Till now, the developed countries hardly knew or bothered about the Indian Auditor General. The UN Audit provided an opportunity to show that the CAG's Organization in India, which was one of the oldest in the world, was second to none. The Indian Audit Teams fanning out across the world and the headquarters officers gave a good account of them and produced audit reports which received widespread appreciation and accolades. The auditing practices followed by the officers of the Department and quality of the audit reports submitted compared favourably with the reports produced by the Auditor Generals of UK, Australia and USA. Now the Auditor General of India was installed on the same pedestal along with the Auditor General of advanced democracies.

The UN Audit made Indian CAG famous, powerful and a globe-trotting emissary. Our CAG who has always been in a dictatorial mould having no accountability became a virtual dictator of a vast organisation and a sole dispenser of patronage. When asked about the criteria for selection of officers for posting to the London and

Washington offices (the overseas offices of the CAG), one of the early CAGs in post-independent India (A. K. Roy) said 'it is sheer patronage'. The same trend of distributing favours and patronage continued forever with increasing starkness. In the matter of selection of officers for the scores of the UN Audit teams, the UN Headquarters and the overseas offices, the CAG became the sole arbiter and would select his favourites for the important assignments. The CAG found it more exciting in attending international meeting and conferences and in visiting the UN offices in various parts of the world, which consumed much of his time and energy.

One offshoot of the UN had been that the CAG's organisation became rich flushed with dollars and a large number of its officers became superrich as compared to their compatriots in other government services. One third of the UN Budget allocated to the UN Board of Auditors was transferred every year to the CAG's Organisation for the Indian CAG to spend according to his best judgement without any interference from the government. The officers in the audit teams and in the New York Office were granted handsome foreign allowances which enabled them to save a major portion after meeting all the expenses. So there was a scramble among the officers to be included in the UN audit teams and the CAG could distribute his patronage according to his discretion.

An unwanted consequence of the preoccupation of CAG's responsibilities with UN audit and international assignments had been that while we tried to show good results to international audience, our own national audit got considerably handicapped and neglected. The majority of the high-performing officers were detailed for the UN audits which affected the quality of audit of the various plans, programmes and schemes of the Central Government and of the state governments. The CAG's Organisation suffered from a shortage of quality staff to effectively conduct performance or value for money audits. For the entire period of eight years when CAG was in charge of UN audits, the focus shifted from national audit to international audit.

VI

Who Leaks the Audit Reports?

A vicious attack on the CAG has recently been launched especially by the Manmohan Singh led UPA government on many fronts because some of the explosive Reports of the CAG had forced the government to bite the dust. In the past, being an important Constitutional Functionary, the Indian CAG had never been criticised by the government or by anybody in the Parliament. This has been the tradition set by Nehru who never allowed any criticism of the

Constitutional Bodies in spite of occasionally having sharp differences and clash of personalities with some of them. Nehru respected the CAG as much as he respected the Judiciary and the Parliament. This healthy tradition was broken into pieces when Manmohan Singh, his ministers and his allies in parliament started a systematic vilification campaign against the CAG's Organization and the CAG himself. There was no reason for doing this except for the fact that his reports hit the vested interests very hard and opened the can of corruption and misdeeds of the two UPA governments. Only once during Vajpayee's time a thing like this happened for some other reason – the ego problem. George Fernandez had been the Defence Minister and he openly challenged the CAG's Audit report on the Kargil War, which pointed out widespread irregularities in procurement of arms and equipment including procurement of unusually heavy and costly aluminium coffins (which could not be used at high altitudes) for transportation of dead soldiers and were procured after the war was over. Funnily, George Fernandez, an extreme egotist, rubbished the entire Audit Report and commissioned a private "expert" to write an alternative audit report which was circulated to all the members of the Parliament. Atal Behari Bajpayee, however, did not give any credence to this report and did not approve of his effort to denigrate CAG's position.

One of the main reasons for the UPA government's discomfiture with the CAG had been the attention the electronic media gave to the CAG's reports. The almost interminable public debate in the TV channels was responsible for bringing the CAG's reports in the public domain and exposed the government's inability and lack of will to curb corruption. Confronted with uncomfortable questions and the flak received from the media, the government started suspecting the CAG for leaking the audit reports to the media who produced copies of audit reports before the Parliament got them. This allegation was found to be one of the most irresponsible statements made without proof against the CAG.

For more than 150 years, the Audit Reports have always been treated as 'secret' documents before they are placed in the Legislature. The moment they are placed on the Table of the House, they become public documents. The question of parliamentary privilege is involved in it; the members of Parliament or of the Legislatures have first right to access the Audit Report and any leakage of the report would be construed as breach of parliamentary privilege. But the fact remains that before TV channels became pro-active, CAG's Audit Reports, however important they could be for the people, were never debated in Parliament or in any public forum. The only forum which discussed the reports was the Public Accounts Committee (PAC) considered to be a mini-Parliament. But the PAC holds its deliberations in camera and members of public and the Press are not allowed to witness the proceedings; moreover, the PAC could discuss a small fraction of the serious objections raised in the Audit Reports. Therefore, the general citizens of the country were hardly aware of the audit reports and their contents which point out governance failures, misuse of tax-payers' money, corrupt practices and performance of various schemes and projects; these are matters which the public are deeply concerned with.

But the situation changed dramatically during the last few years which witnessed a virtual revolution in Information Technology, Electronic Media, Internet and public consciousness. CAG's Audit Reports (about 100 reports published each year for the Central and the State Governments) contain a mine of information which the TV channels are exploiting for the benefit of the public. In a fiercely competitive world of the electronic media, each media house establishes its own system of 'reliable sources,' by fair or unfair means to filter secret information. These days, the hackers are able to enter any website or computer system and can retrieve any information. In order to be the 'first' or 'exclusive' in breaking news, the TV channels manage to get hold of excerpts of the Audit Reports before they are actually placed in Parliament. Not having any clue, the government tends to point finger at the CAG's

Office every time there is a leakage of his reports, but the unfounded allegation was always aimed at showing the CAG in bad light.

The government knows more than anybody else that the Audit Reports are a culmination of a lengthy process of interaction between the government and the Audit Office starting from inspection of government establishments by the audit parties and ending with the submission of the printed reports to the President of India who causes them to be laid on the Tables of both Houses of Parliament through the Ministry of Finance. In the case of the States, the reports are submitted to the Governor who causes them to be laid on the Table of the State legislature. In between, there are several stages of consultations with the departments, which extend for a year and in some cases for several years. The process involves issue of the Inspection Report, issue of important audit objections, getting reply and explanations from t government, settlement of issues on the basis of reply and issue of the 'Draft Para' to the government. 'Draft Para' proposed to be included in the Audit Report is always issued to the Secretary of the Department asking for the comments of the government at highest level. The Audit reports are given a final shape and sent for printing only after receiving the final comments from the government. In several cases, replies are not received from the government even after a long wait and in such cases, it is presumed that the government accepts the contention of the Audit Office. It will be noticed that during the whole exercise, several copies of the draft audit report or the 'Draft Para' would be available at various levels of the government who may not strictly treat them as secret documents. According to the Rules of Business, it is the responsibility of the Ministry of Finance to include the task of submission of the Audit Reports in the schedule of business of the Parliament and in this matter, more often than not, top priority is not accorded and as a result, copies of Audit Reports awaiting submission languish for several days, even weeks, in the Ministry of Finance. The possibility of leakage of the Reports to media either from the concerned administrative ministry or from the Ministry of Finance or during transit enhances considerably with each day of delay in reaching all the copies (about 800 copies) in the Parliament House. In modern days, leaking like whistle blowing should not be made a major issue; the government should be more sensitive and appreciative of what has been written in the Audit Reports and initiate immediate remedial action in a transparent manner, which would be a test of the triumph of democracy.

About the Author

A product of Presidency College (now Presidency University), Parimal Brahma, poet, writer and singer started his early life as a Lecturer in Economics before he joined the Central Civil Services by sheer accident. The glamour and demands of the Civil Service muted a promising poet and singer. While the author rose to the highest level of bureaucracy, he always felt he was a misfit in the system and described himself as a 'non-conformist idiot'. As a participant-observer, he had seen many a drama played on the corridors of power. In this book, in his unique humorous style, he has tried to play back and retell some of the funny tales and episodes witnessed on the stages of our great democracy. While working in various Central Ministries, the author discovered that the majority of the political bosses were out to subvert constitutional functioning making non-transparent methodologies as part of their natural behaviour. While all the major decisions are taken by the ministers, they are not accountable to the Public Accounts Committee of Parliament, in fact to anybody and the burden of their misdeeds always fall on the bureaucrats. Honest bureaucrats who assert themselves for transparency and constitutionality are either crushed or sidetracked. Honesty, integrity, discipline and patriotism are anathema to the present breed of politicians and are perhaps incompatible with the present stage of our democracy.